BEARING WITNESS FOR

GAZA

KIERAN BEVILLE

DB DUBLIN
BOOK PUBLISHING

Block 4 Harcourt Rd,
Saint Kevin's, Dublin,
D02 HW77, Ireland

Copyright © 2025 Kieran Beville

ISBN (Paperback)
ISBN (Hardback)

TABLE OF CONTENTS

ABOUT THE AUTHOR

Dr Kieran Beville is an Irish poet, author and former educator whose career spans literature, philosophical theology, and intercultural engagement.

A former teacher of English and History, he was also a tutor at University College Cork, Ireland in the 1980s and later a professor in the Intercultural Studies Department at Tyndale Theological Seminary, Amsterdam, where he taught Master classes (M.Div and M.Th).

His teaching and leadership training work has brought him to Eastern Europe, the Middle East and India, fostering dialogue across cultural and ideological divides.

Beville is the author of over twenty books across genres – from creative writing guides and biographies to poetry and works on faith and culture – published in Ireland, the UK, USA and India. He has seven collections of poetry and many of these poems have also appeared in literary journals and anthologies worldwide.

A regular newspaper columnist and feature writer, Beville's work often spotlights local artists, musicians and writers, reflecting his commitment to cultural heritage and human stories.

Formerly a Baptist pastor and author of numerous theological books and articles, he left the evangelical community in 2017 and embraced his voice as a secular poet and writer.

Through decades of writing, teaching and travel, Dr Beville has borne witness to the human condition across continents and communities, bringing a perspective shaped by history, cultural awareness and human connection.

SETTING THE STAGE

This is a brief overview introducing the book's purpose, scope, and significance. It frames the complex crisis in Gaza and the broader geopolitical, humanitarian, and moral questions explored throughout the text.

PART I: HISTORICAL ROOTS AND HUMANITARIAN CRISIS

The devastation of Gaza cannot be understood in isolation from its past. This section traces the origins of today's crisis, starting with the 1917 Balfour Declaration—when a colonial power pledged support for a "national home for the Jewish people" in Palestine, disregarding the political rights of its indigenous Arab population. We then explore the legacy of colonialism, the 1948 Nakba, decades of occupation, and the blockade that has shaped daily life in Gaza for over 15 years. This section goes beyond statistics to show the human cost—refugee camps, collapsed hospitals, and the endurance of a people under siege.

1. **FROM THE BALFOUR DECLARATION TO GAZA** – How a Century-Old Promise Shapes a Modern Humanitarian Crisis.

2. **OCCUPATION, BLOCKADE AND RESISTANCE** – Tracing the Historical Roots of Gaza's Catastrophe.

3. **THE HAMAS OCTOBER 7 ATTACK** – Context and Pretext for Israel's Destruction of Gaza.

4. **HUMANITARIAN CRISIS IN GAZA** – Challenges and the Global Response.

5. **AID IN GAZA** – Targeting Humanitarian Workers and the Collapse of Protection.

6. **A CATALOGUE OF HORROR** – Human Rights Violations and Suffering.

7. **RESISTANCE, REFUGEES, AND RUBBLE** – Gaza's Struggle for Survival.

8. **YOUTH AND EDUCATION IN GAZA** – Life Interrupted by War.

PART II: LEGAL, MORAL, AND POLITICAL QUESTIONS

Is Gaza a site of genocide or self-defence? Do states built on displacement have the right to exist unchanged? What is the cost of silence from powerful allies? These chapters tackle the moral dilemmas and legal complexities at the heart of Gaza, questioning the legitimacy of old paradigms and exposing the failures of international law to protect the vulnerable.

1. **GENOCIDE OR SELF-DEFENCE?** – Testing Israel's War against Gaza under International Law.

2. **ISRAEL'S DEVASTATION OF GAZA** – The Inescapable Verdict of Genocide and War Crimes.

3. **HUMAN SHIELDS AND HUMAN COSTS** – Myths and Realities of Urban Warfare in Gaza.

4. **AMERICA'S COMPLICITY** – How U.S. Foreign Policy Enables Atrocities in Gaza.

5. **DRAGGED INTO THE ABYSS** - How Israel's Genocidal War on Gaza Reveals America's Moral Depravity.

6. **EUROPE'S DEAFENING SILENCE** – The EU's Failure to Condemn Israel's War Crimes in Gaza.

7. **GERMANY'S MORAL COLLAPSE** – Complicity in the Gaza Genocide.

8. **SILENT PARTNERS IN WAR** – The UK's Complicity in Gaza's Ordeal.

PART III: GLOBAL CONSEQUENCES AND GEOPOLITICS

Gaza is not just a local tragedy; it reshapes alliances, exposes double standards, and tests the credibility of international law. This part explores how the conflict affects regional dynamics, how American power shields impunity, and how social media plays a role in the battle for truth. It shows how Gaza's suffering also highlights deeper global crises of justice, order, and conscience.

PART IV: SILENCING, MEMORY, AND THE BATTLE FOR NARRATIVE

Beyond bombs and blockades lies another battle: over words, images, and collective memory. From poets silenced by publishers to journalists barred from Gaza, and the living trauma of the Nakba carried through generations, these chapters explore how narrative is controlled—and why remembrance itself becomes an act of resistance. They address the dangers of silence in the face of injustice, drawing powerful parallels between historical moments of moral failures and today's widespread inaction.

This section asks: whose voices are heard, whose stories remain untold, and what happens when truth itself is under siege?

CONCLUSION – TOWARDS JUSTICE AND PEACE

The conclusion ties together the complex histories, legal questions, and human stories explored in the book. It urges reflection on the cost of silence and complicity, highlights the resilience of Gaza's people, and calls for urgent, inclusive solutions that prioritise human dignity and accountability. This final section challenges readers to engage beyond the pages, embracing the moral responsibility to speak, remember, and act.

INTRODUCTION

The devastating conflict in Gaza stands as one of the most severe humanitarian crises of our time, marked by immense human suffering, widespread destruction, and deep political complexity. This collection of chapters, *Bearing Witness For Gaza*, sheds light on the multifaceted realities of Gaza—from the devastating toll on civilians, including the disproportionate impact on women and children, to the systemic erosion of rights under an enduring blockade and repeated military assaults.

The collapse of Gaza's already fragile health and infrastructure systems, compounded by psychological trauma and shortages of essential resources, paints a grim picture of a population trapped in an endless cycle of violence and deprivation.

But these tragedies cannot be understood in isolation. They are deeply rooted in a long and contested history of occupation, displacement, and competing national aspirations that stretches back over a century. A pivotal moment in this history was the **Balfour Declaration of 1917**, in which the British government expressed support for "the establishment in Palestine of a national home for the Jewish people", while notably failing to secure the political and civil rights of the Arab majority already living there. This declaration, issued in the context of colonial strategy and wartime diplomacy, set off decades of tension, dispossession, and conflict, the effects of which are still acutely felt today.

The Nakba and ongoing displacement are living traumas that shape Palestinian identity and resistance. The blockade, political fragmentation, and failed peace efforts have created a crisis that transcends local borders, reverberating through regional geopolitics and global diplomacy. Meanwhile, international responses have been marked by stark contradictions: powerful nations provide military aid and diplomatic support that many argue amount to complicity in ongoing violations, while global institutions struggle to hold perpetrators accountable.

This debate goes beyond immediate violence to raise deep legal and moral questions. Is Israel's military campaign one of self-defence or genocide? How does international law apply in a densely populated urban conflict zone? These questions are amplified in real time on social media and digital documentation, which bring the human stories of Gaza's residents—stories of fear, resilience, and hope—into global consciousness even as censorship, media blockades, and political pressures silence many voices. The suppression of poets, journalists, and activists further distorts public understanding, underscoring the ongoing struggle over who controls the narrative and how history itself is told.

This volume also examines the shifting tide of global public opinion, as images and testimonies challenge long-held assumptions and inspire growing demands for justice, accountability, and the protection of fundamental human rights. The voices of Gaza's youth, educators, and cultural leaders remind us that, even amid the rubble and blockade, a determined spirit of survival and resistance endures. At the same time, the suppression of pro-Palestinian speech and protest in many Western democracies raises urgent questions about the state of free expression and democratic values worldwide.

Together, these chapters offer a detailed and comprehensive examination of Gaza's ongoing catastrophe—its human costs, historical roots, geopolitical consequences, and the urgent need for principled international action. They urge readers to confront uncomfortable truths, break the silence, and engage with the moral imperative to uphold dignity, justice, and peace for all those affected by this tragic conflict.

PART-I
HISTORICAL ROOTS AND HUMANITARIAN CRISIS

FROM THE BALFOUR DECLARATION TO GAZA

How a Century-old Promise Shapes a Modern Humanitarian Crisis

In the annals of modern Middle Eastern history, few documents have had as deep and lasting an impact as the Balfour Declaration. Issued on 2 November 1917 by Britain's then Foreign Secretary Arthur James Balfour, it was a short letter addressed to Lord Walter Rothschild, a leader of the British Jewish community. Despite its brevity, it set the stage for decades of conflict, displacement, and contested identities in the land known then as Palestine—a land that is now shared, disputed, and fought over by Israelis and Palestinians.

The declaration famously stated that "His Majesty's Government view with favour the establishment in Palestine of a national home for the Jewish people," but also included a caveat: "nothing shall be done which may prejudice the civil and religious rights of existing non-Jewish communities in Palestine." At first glance, the declaration attempted to balance these two competing commitments. In practice, however, it ignited a process that would radically alter Palestine's demographic and political landscape, sowing seeds of resentment and conflict that still reverberate—most painfully visible today, especially in the Gaza Strip.

IMPERIAL INTERESTS AND IDEOLOGICAL CURRENTS

To understand why Britain issued the Balfour Declaration, it's essential to look at the geopolitical chessboard of World War I. At the time, the Ottoman Empire still controlled Palestine. Britain, eager to weaken the Ottomans and secure its own post-war influence in the Middle East, saw supporting Zionist aspirations as a strategic advantage. British leaders believed it would help gain the support of Jewish communities in the United States and Russia for the Allied war effort.

The declaration was also influenced by the ideological trends of the time, particularly the Zionist movement that emerged in the late 19th century under figures like Theodor Herzl. Zionism called for the creation of a national home for Jews fleeing persecution in Europe, with Palestine identified as the chosen land based on historical and religious narratives. However, this vision largely disregarded the fact that Palestine was already home to an established Arab population, whose own political and national aspirations were side-lined in the process.

For Britain, then, supporting Zionism was not only a moral or ideological gesture but also a pragmatic move to secure imperial interests in the Eastern Mediterranean and protect access to the Suez Canal, a vital maritime route to British colonies in Asia.

Yet, conspicuously absent from the diplomatic conversations that produced the Balfour Declaration were the Arab inhabitants of Palestine, who made up about 90% of the population at the time. Their voices were neither solicited nor heard. This absence of consultation would become a defining feature of the conflicts that followed.

Mandate, Migration, and Mounting Tensions

After World War I and the dissolution of the Ottoman Empire, the League of Nations awarded Britain the Mandate for Palestine in 1922. This mandate required Britain to implement the Balfour Declaration, effectively turning it into official policy. This led to a significant increase in Jewish immigration to Palestine, particularly as Jews fled rising antisemitism in Europe during the 1920s and 1930s.

For the Palestinian Arab population, this influx of immigrants threatened not only economic stability but also their cultural and political self-determination. Land sales to Jewish immigrants—sometimes encouraged by absentee landlords—led to the displacement of Arab tenant farmers. Tensions grew, resulting in violent clashes between Arab and Jewish communities, culminating in major confrontations like the Arab revolt of 1936–1939.

Britain, caught between its commitment to Zionist aspirations and the reality of Arab resistance, found itself unable to satisfy either side fully. The White Paper of 1939 attempted to limit Jewish immigration and land purchases. It angered Zionists and failed to appease Arab leaders, who sought full independence. As World War II approached, tensions in Palestine remained unresolved.

The Nakba and the Birth of Israel

The end of World War II brought new urgency to the question of Palestine. The horrors of the Holocaust galvanised global sympathy for Jewish survivors, many of whom sought to immigrate to Palestine. Britain, weakened by the war and unable to manage the mounting conflict, referred the matter to the newly formed United Nations.

In 1947, the UN proposed a partition plan to divide Palestine into separate Jewish and Arab states, with Jerusalem placed under international administration. Jewish leaders accepted the plan, albeit reluctantly, while Arab leaders rejected it, arguing that it violated the rights of the majority Arab population.

On 14 May 1948, David Ben-Gurion declared the establishment of the State of Israel. The following day, neighbouring Arab states invaded, marking the start of the first Arab-Israeli war. By the war's end, Israel controlled territory beyond that allocated in the UN partition plan. An estimated 700,000 Palestinians fled or were expelled from their homes—a mass displacement Palestinians refer to as the Nakba, or "catastrophe." Many of these refugees settled in Gaza, which was then under Egyptian control, transforming it into a dense patchwork of refugee camps.

GAZA: FROM REFUGEE CAMPS TO BLOCKADE

Originally a quiet coastal strip of fishing villages and farmland, Gaza's fate was fundamentally altered by the events of 1948. The arrival of hundreds of thousands of refugees transformed it into one of the most densely populated places on Earth. In 1967, after the Six-Day War, Israel occupied Gaza along with the West Bank, East Jerusalem, and other territories.

The decades that followed saw Gaza become a focal point of the broader Israeli-Palestinian conflict. Israeli settlements were established in the strip, deepening Palestinian grievances. In 1993, the Oslo Accords raised hopes for a two-state solution, and the Palestinian Authority was established as an interim self-governing body. However, progress faltered as mutual distrust and violence persisted.

In 2005, Israel unilaterally withdrew its settlers and military from Gaza, but maintained control over its borders, airspace, and coastline. A year later, Hamas, a political and militant Islamist group, won the Palestinian legislative elections. In 2007, after violent clashes with the rival Fatah faction, Hamas took full control of Gaza. Israel and Egypt responded by imposing a blockade, citing security concerns over Hamas rocket attacks.

Today, Gaza's 2.2 million residents live under the weight of this blockade, facing chronic shortages of clean water, electricity, and medical supplies. More than half of the population are descendants of refugees from 1948—a legacy of the Balfour Declaration and the conflicts it set in motion.

THE HUMAN TOLL AND THE HISTORICAL SHADOW

The humanitarian crisis in Gaza is severe and persistent. According to UN agencies, youth unemployment exceeds 60%. The majority of the population relies on humanitarian aid, and essential infrastructure—such as sewage systems and hospitals—operates on the brink of collapse. Periodic conflicts between Israel and Hamas further devastated civilian life, destroying homes, schools, and hospitals.

For many Palestinians, the Balfour Declaration is more than just a historical document. It symbolises the moment when a foreign power promised their land to another people, disregarding their rights and political aspirations. It marks, in their view, the beginning of dispossession that culminated in the Nakba and continues today in the form of occupation and blockade.

For many Israelis, by contrast, the declaration is seen as a vital step toward the establishment of a safe haven after centuries of persecution culminating in the Holocaust. From this perspective, the document was an acknowledgment of the Jewish people's historical connection to the land and their right to self-determination.

These contrasting narratives remain deeply embedded in the identities of both peoples and continue to shape political discourse, making compromise elusive.

WHY HISTORY STILL MATTERS

The continuing relevance of the Balfour Declaration shows how deeply historical promises—and the ways they are interpreted—shape present realities. The declaration's failure to clearly define the rights of the Arab population created a vacuum that, over time, fuelled cycles of conflict and mistrust.

Attempts at resolving the Israeli-Palestinian conflict often fail not only due to practical issues such as borders and security, but also over these competing historical narratives. For Palestinians in Gaza and beyond, recognition of the injustice they associate with the Balfour Declaration and the Nakba remains a central demand. For Israelis, acknowledgment of their historical connection to the land and their right to safety is equally important.

The humanitarian crisis in Gaza cannot be separated from these deeper historical currents. The blockade and repeated wars are symptoms of a conflict rooted in questions left unanswered in 1917: who has a rightful claim to the land, and how can two peoples with deeply held historical ties share it?

A Century Later: Toward Accountability and Hope

As the world marks over a century since the Balfour Declaration, there are growing calls for reflection and accountability. Some historians and activists argue that Britain holds moral responsibility for the ongoing conflict, having issued a promise without adequately safeguarding the rights of the existing Arab population. Others emphasise that responsibility now lies with current leaders on all sides to negotiate a fair and lasting peace.

What is clear is that the legacy of the Balfour Declaration cannot simply be consigned to the history books. It continues to shape the physical, political, and psychological landscape in which Israelis and Palestinians live today.

For Gaza, the challenge is especially urgent. Its people live not only with daily material hardship, but also with the burden of historical dispossession and the feeling of being trapped by decisions made long before they were born. Yet many in Gaza still hope for a future where the blockade ends, political reconciliation becomes possible, and dignity is restored.

A century after Britain's fateful promise, the need to address its consequences—through dialogue, empathy, and political courage—remains as urgent as ever. The story of Gaza, seen through the lens of the Balfour Declaration, is ultimately a story about how the past continues to define the present—and how acknowledging that past could be the first step toward a different future.

Occupation, Blockade, and Resistance

Tracing the Historical Roots of Gaza's Catastrophe

To understand Gaza, you have to look past the smoke of war and see the centuries-old scars beneath. In the summer heat, Gaza's shattered skyline tells a story that didn't begin with the latest bombing campaign. The rubble, the mourning families, the hospitals overflowing with the wounded — they speak not only of an immediate disaster, but of a catastrophe generations in the making. To many outside observers, the war looks like an eruption; to Palestinians, it is the latest chapter in a long, grim history of dispossession, blockade, and resistance.

This is the story of Gaza not as a crisis that appeared from nowhere, but as the tragic consequence of historical forces converging over decades: colonial legacies, military occupation, and a policy of isolation that has turned a strip of land into an open-air prison.

A Land Carved by Empire

Long before Gaza was headline news, it was a crossroads of empires. Ancient Egyptians, Romans, Byzantines, Ottomans, and finally the British all ruled over this narrow coastal territory. For centuries, its people lived off trade, fishing, and agriculture, moving freely along the Mediterranean coast.

But Gaza's modern suffering truly began in the 20th century, with the collapse of the Ottoman Empire and the carving up of the Middle East into British and French mandates. In 1947, the UN proposed partitioning Palestine into Jewish and Arab states, a plan Palestinians

22

overwhelmingly rejected as unjust. In the war that followed Israel's declaration of independence in 1948, more than 700,000 Palestinians were expelled or fled their homes in what they call the Nakba — the "catastrophe."

Many of those refugees poured into Gaza, which was then under Egyptian administration. Their descendants still live there today, often in overcrowded camps, waiting for a right of return that has never materialised.

OCCUPATION AND THE SEEDS OF RESISTANCE

In 1967, during the Six-Day War, Israel captured Gaza from Egypt and the West Bank from Jordan, beginning a military occupation that continues, in different forms, to this day. For years, Israeli settlements spread across Gaza's fertile land, guarded by soldiers. Palestinian resistance movements grew, fuelled by frustration and the demand for liberation.

Hamas, now internationally known, emerged in the late 1980s as an offshoot of Egypt's Muslim Brotherhood during the First Intifada — a mass Palestinian uprising against Israeli rule. Unlike the secular Fatah movement, Hamas blended nationalism with political Islam, gaining support partly through extensive social welfare programmes in Gaza's impoverished neighbourhoods.

By the 1990s, the Oslo Accords offered a fragile hope of peace, creating the Palestinian Authority and sketching a pathway to a two-state solution. But for Gaza, little changed. Settlements expanded, economic restrictions tightened, and Israeli forces remained.

When the Second Intifada broke out in 2000, violence escalated. Suicide bombings, military invasions, and targeted assassinations hardened attitudes on both sides. In 2005, Israel unilaterally withdrew its settlers and soldiers from inside Gaza, but kept control over its borders, airspace, and sea — effectively maintaining the siege.

The Blockade: Gaza Turns Into a Prison

In 2006, Hamas won a surprise victory in Palestinian legislative elections. A year later, after a brief and bloody conflict with Fatah, Hamas seized control of Gaza. Israel, along with Egypt, imposed a strict blockade. Basic goods trickled in; exports nearly stopped. Electricity became unreliable, and Gaza's economy collapsed.

The blockade was meant to weaken Hamas, but its greatest victims were ordinary Palestinians. Today, more than 80% of Gaza's population depends on humanitarian aid. Unemployment hovers around 50%. Clean water is scarce, hospitals run on generators, and young people see little future.

Israel justifies the blockade as necessary to prevent Hamas from acquiring weapons. Critics, including UN agencies and human rights organisations, call it collective punishment — illegal under international law.

Wars, Ceasefires, and Ruins

Since Hamas took over Gaza, the territory has been trapped in a cycle of conflict. Major Israeli military operations — in 2008–09, 2012, 2014, 2021, and now — have killed thousands, including many civilians. Rockets launched by Palestinian armed groups have killed dozens in Israel and keep millions living in fear.

In each war, Gaza's infrastructure — homes, schools, hospitals — is reduced further to rubble. Reconstruction is slow or blocked by the siege. Even before the latest escalation, the UN warned Gaza would soon become "unliveable."

Israel argues its strikes target militants embedded among civilians. But with Gaza's population density among the world's highest, avoiding civilian casualties is nearly impossible. Human rights groups accuse both Israel and Palestinian factions of war crimes: indiscriminate rocket fire on Israel, and disproportionate bombing in Gaza.

THE FORGOTTEN REFUGEES

Beyond geopolitics, Gaza's tragedy is rooted in unresolved refugee claims. Nearly 70% of Gaza's population are refugees or their descendants of refugees from 1948. The demand for the right of return remains central to Palestinian identity, but has no place in Israeli political discourse, where it is seen as a demographic threat.

In refugee camps like Jabalia and Beach Camp, generations have grown up knowing only crowded alleys, concrete shelters, and stories of villages they've never seen. For them, the struggle is not just over Gaza's present, but its past.

RESISTANCE: VIOLENCE AND NONVIOLENCE

In Western media, Gaza's resistance is often seen only through the lens of rockets and tunnels. But Gaza is also home to activists, journalists, and artists who risk arrest and bombing to speak out. The Great March of Return in 2018 saw tens of thousands protest peacefully along the border fence, demanding the right of return and an end to the blockade. Israeli snipers killed more than 200 and wounded thousands, drawing international criticism.

Yet these non-violent movements rarely make headlines like rockets and airstrikes do. In the global imagination, Gaza's story remains trapped in images of violence.

COLONIAL LEGACIES AND GLOBAL SILENCE

Gaza's suffering is not just local; it is part of a broader history of colonialism and selective solidarity. The borders that confine Palestinians were drawn by British and French diplomats who never imagined the people who would live behind them. International law, built partly to prevent atrocities after the Second World War, has so far failed Gaza.

The US remains Israel's strongest ally, providing billions in military aid. European governments often condemn violence "on both sides," but rarely act. Meanwhile, the Arab world, once vocal, is now divided by its own crises and distracted by normalisation deals with Israel.

A CATASTROPHE – GENERATIONS IN THE MAKING

Today's war, like those before it, will likely end in rubble, grief, and an uneasy ceasefire. But without addressing the deeper roots — occupation, blockade, dispossession — peace will remain impossible.

As Gaza's children sleep under bombardment, their lives shaped by forces older than their grandparents, the world faces a choice: to see Gaza's catastrophe as an unavoidable tragedy or as the outcome of policies, decisions, and historical injustices that can still be changed.

"If you want to understand Gaza," says historian Rashid Khalidi, "you have to understand that it is not just about Hamas or rockets. It is about a century of colonialism, displacement, and resistance."

Until those truths are confronted, Gaza will remain what it has become: a symbol of a broken world order, where justice remains a promise too often betrayed.

THE HAMAS OCTOBER 7 ATTACK

Context and Pretext for Israel's Destruction of Gaza

On 7 October 2023, the world witnessed a shocking escalation in the long-running Israeli–Palestinian conflict when Hamas, the Islamist militant group that governs the Gaza Strip, launched a large-scale, coordinated attack against Israel. Thousands of militants infiltrated Israeli towns near the Gaza border, firing thousands of rockets and engaging in brutal close-quarters fighting. This unprecedented assault resulted in the deaths of over 1,400 Israelis — civilians and soldiers — dead, with hundreds more injured or abducted.

The scale and ferocity of the attack stunned Israel and the international community. It shattered a fragile calm that had lasted for years and sent Israel into a state of national emergency. Yet, as devastating as the attack was, it also marked a turning point: it became the political and military pretext for Israel's subsequent destruction of Gaza, a campaign whose repercussions are still unfolding.

To understand the complex and tragic dynamics at play, it is essential to analyse how the Hamas attack functioned not only as a brutal act of violence but also as the trigger for an overwhelming Israeli response.

HISTORICAL BACKGROUND: THE LONG SHADOW OF CONFLICT

The Israeli–Palestinian conflict is one of the most protracted and complex disputes of the modern era. The Gaza Strip, a densely populated coastal enclave home to nearly two million Palestinians, has been under Israeli blockade since 2007, when Hamas seized control from the Palestinian Authority. Israel and Egypt have maintained tight restrictions on the movement of people and goods, citing security concerns. Hamas, meanwhile, is designated a terrorist organisation by Israel, the US, and the EU.

Since 2007, Gaza has endured repeated rounds of intense fighting between Israel and Hamas, including major conflicts in 2008–09, 2012, 2014, and smaller escalations since. Each conflict has left thousands of Palestinians dead and Gaza's already fragile infrastructure in ruins, deepening the humanitarian crisis.

Despite periodic ceasefires and international calls for peace, the underlying political issues remain unresolved: Palestinians seek sovereignty and an end to occupation, while Israel insists on security guarantees. Gaza, cut off from the West Bank and much of the outside world, remains a powder keg.

THE OCTOBER 7 HAMAS ATTACK: A TACTICAL AND SYMBOLIC SHOCK

On October 7, Hamas launched what it called its operation "Al-Aqsa Flood" — a meticulously planned surprise assault with multiple elements:

- **Rocket barrage**: More than 5,000 rockets were fired into southern and central Israel within hours, overwhelming early warning systems.

- **Ground infiltrations**: Militants breached the heavily fortified border fence, entering Israeli towns such as Sderot, Nir Oz, and communities in the Eshkol region. They carried out shootings, kidnappings, and attacks on civilians.

- **Hostage taking**: Over 200 Israelis, both soldiers and civilians, were abducted to be used as bargaining chips.

- **Civilian massacres**: Many victims were massacred in their homes, schools, and shelters — acts of brutality that shocked Israel and the wider world.

The attack was the deadliest on Israeli soil in decades and marked a dramatic escalation. Israeli officials and much of the global community condemned Hamas for the deliberate targeting of civilians.

ISRAEL'S MILITARY RESPONSE: FROM DEFENCE TO DESTRUCTION

Israel's reaction was immediate and overwhelming. The Israeli government declared a state of war and launched "Operation Iron Swords," a massive military campaign aimed at crippling Hamas and securing the release of hostages. The campaign has involved:

- **Extensive airstrikes**: Thousands of strikes against Hamas's military infrastructure, tunnels, weapons depots, and leadership figures.

- **Ground operations:** The Israeli Defence Forces (IDF) mobilised for potential ground incursions, focused on dismantling Hamas's networks.

- **Tightened siege**: Israel intensified the blockade, cutting off electricity, water, and fuel to Gaza, worsening humanitarian conditions.

- **Civilian impact**: Despite Israel's claims of targeting militants, the campaign has caused massive civilian casualties and destroyed homes, schools, hospitals, and vital infrastructure.

CONTEXT: WHY THE ATTACK HAPPENED

To understand — though not to justify — why Hamas launched the 7 October attack, one has to look beyond the immediate violence to the deeper context of occupation, blockade, and failed peace efforts:

1. **Prolonged siege**: The Israeli–Egyptian blockade has strangled Gaza's economy and restricted basic resources for over 15 years, creating poverty, unemployment, and despair.

2. **Political stalemate**: Repeated failures to establish a viable Palestinian state or meaningful autonomy have fuelled frustration. Hamas positions itself as a movement of resistance against occupation.

3. **Cycles of violence**: Each Israeli military operation leaves Gaza more devastated, creating fertile ground for radicalisation and recruitment.

4. **Regional shifts:** Normalisation deals between Israel and Arab states, along with US policies, have altered the regional balance, influencing Hamas's calculations.

The October 7 attack was condemned worldwide, but it cannot be separated from this broader context of systemic oppression and unresolved conflict.

The 7 October attack gave Israel both the justification and political cover to escalate its military campaign to unprecedented levels. Key elements of how the attack has functioned as a pretext include:

1. National security and public opinion

The shock and horror of the Hamas attack galvanised Israeli public opinion in favour of a harsh response. The government presented the offensive as a matter of existential survival, framing Gaza as a terrorist enclave that had to be neutralised. This allowed Israel's leadership to secure broad domestic and international backing for the military campaign.

2. International diplomacy and legal narrative

Israel has emphasised its right to self-defence under international law, citing Hamas's deliberate targeting of civilians. This framing has limited international criticism and deflected calls for restraint. The attack has been used to justify measures that would otherwise be widely condemned, such as large-scale bombings and blockades.

3. Military strategy: decapitating Hamas

The attack provided the impetus for Israel to pursue the "complete dismantling" of Hamas's military capabilities and leadership. Its scale was cited as evidence that partial or limited operations would be insufficient.

4. Humanitarian cost as collateral damage

Israel insists that civilian casualties are unfortunate but inevitable in the fight against terrorism embedded in densely populated areas. The brutality of the attack has been used to downplay or justify the humanitarian catastrophe in Gaza.

HUMANITARIAN CONSEQUENCES: GAZA ON THE BRINK

The consequences for Gaza have been catastrophic:

- **Casualties**: Tens of thousands of Palestinians, mostly civilians (women and children), have been killed or injured.

- **Infrastructure**: Power plants, water facilities, hospitals, and schools have been destroyed or severely damaged.

- **Displacement**: More than half of Gaza's population has been forced from their homes, many sheltering in overcrowded facilities.

- **Health crisis**: Medical supplies are critically low, while access to clean water and sanitation is severely compromised.

International aid organisations have warned of an impending humanitarian disaster, but calls for a ceasefire and greater relief access have largely gone unmet.

CRITIQUES AND CONTROVERSIES

The aftermath of the 7 October attack and Israel's response has sparked intense debate:

- **Proportionality and collective punishment**: Critics argue that Israel's military campaign amounts to collective punishment of Gaza's civilian population, violating international humanitarian law.

- **Cycle of violence**: Many see the escalation as perpetuating a vicious cycle, laying the groundwork for future conflict.

- **Peace prospects**: The devastation may further diminish hopes for a negotiated peace or a two-state solution.

- **Accountability**: Questions remain over responsibility for civilian deaths on both sides and the need for impartial investigations.

A TRAGIC ESCALATION FUELLED BY HISTORY AND POLITICS

The Hamas attack of 7 October was a horrific and unprecedented assault that plunged the Israeli–Palestinian conflict into a new and deadly phase. It was both a brutal act of war and the pretext that enabled Israel to launch a massive military campaign against Gaza. Yet to fully understand the tragedy unfolding, one must look beyond the immediate violence to the deeper historical grievances, political failures, and humanitarian crises underpinning the conflict.

Israel's destruction of Gaza is not only a military response but part of a wider strategy shaped by decades of conflict and occupation. The consequences are devastating for civilians on both sides and underline the urgent need for renewed commitment to dialogue, justice, and peace — without which the cycle of violence will inevitably continue.

HUMANITARIAN CRISIS IN GAZA

Challenges and Global Response

Tucked along the Mediterranean coast, Gaza is often defined in global consciousness by its conflicts and blockades. But beyond the headlines lies a persistent humanitarian catastrophe that has, for years, shaped daily life for its more than two million residents. The crisis in Gaza is not just about moments of intense violence; it is a continuous struggle shaped by economic isolation, chronic shortages, and the immense human cost of political deadlock.

This chapter examines the dimensions of Gaza's humanitarian crisis: the living conditions of civilians, the impact of prolonged blockades, and the often fraught global response. It also considers how aid efforts attempt to bridge the gaps — and why lasting solutions remain elusive despite decades of international attention.

LIFE UNDER BLOCKADE: A CRISIS THAT TOUCHES EVERY ASPECT OF DAILY LIVING

Since 2007, when Hamas took control of Gaza, Israel — supported in part by Egypt — has imposed a land, air, and sea blockade on the territory. Intended to restrict weapons and weaken Hamas's military capacity, the blockade has had sweeping consequences for ordinary people.

The economic impact is stark: unemployment in Gaza has hovered around 45–50%, among the highest in the world. For young people, the picture is even bleaker, with youth unemployment often exceeding

60%. Many university graduates spend years searching for work, often without success.

The blockade has also strangled trade and industry. Gaza once exported textiles, furniture, and produce, contributing to a modest but diverse economy. Today, industries operate at a fraction of their capacity, hampered by restrictions on the import of raw materials and the export of goods.

But it is in the basics of daily life that the crisis is most acute:

- **Electricity**: Gaza's power plants, heavily dependent on imported fuel, cannot meet demand. Residents endure rolling blackouts, often receiving only four to eight hours of power a day. This disrupts everything from water pumps to hospital equipment.

- **Clean water**: More than 90% of water from Gaza's coastal aquifer is unfit for human consumption, contaminated by sewage, seawater intrusion, and overuse. Families rely on costly water trucks or small desalination plants, which themselves require constant electricity.

- **Healthcare**: The blockade restricts medical supplies and spare parts for hospital equipment. Facilities face chronic shortages, and while medical staff are highly skilled, they struggle to provide even basic care. Patients often need permits to leave Gaza for specialised treatment — permits that are not always granted.

These challenges intensify during military escalations, when infrastructure is destroyed and aid convoys struggle to reach those in need.

The Toll on Civilians: Beyond Statistics

Numbers can tell part of the story — unemployment rates, hospital shortages, calories per capita. But behind each statistic lies a daily reality of anxiety and resilience.

Children, who make up nearly half of Gaza's population, grow up surrounded by the sights and sounds of conflict: drones buzzing overhead, damaged buildings, and families speaking in hushed tones about possible attacks. Many experience psychological trauma, expressed through depression, suicidal thoughts, nightmares, bedwetting, and difficulty concentrating at school.

Parents often describe a sense of helplessness. Even as they try to shield their children, the structural limitations of life under blockade leave them with few options. Young people, despite their education and ambition, face a future defined not by possibility but by borders they cannot cross.

The crisis affects even the basics of family life. Weddings are scaled back due to economic hardship, while funerals are heartbreakingly common after major escalations. Everyday life continues, but always under the shadow of constraint and uncertainty.

The Role of Aid: Lifeline and Limitation

In the absence of normal economic activity and movement, aid has become essential for Gaza's survival. The United Nations Relief and Works Agency (UNRWA) plays a particularly crucial role, providing education, healthcare, food aid, and employment to hundreds of thousands of Palestinian refugees.

UNRWA

The United Nations Relief and Works Agency is still active in Gaza, despite facing major obstacles

CURRENT ACTIVITIES

The agency remains a lifeline for millions in Gaza, providing food assistance, healthcare, psychosocial support, education, shelter, and essential water and sanitation services. By late February 2025, UNRWA had distributed food to around two million people, managed 120 shelters, facilitated over 360,000 health consultations, and supplied non-food items to about half a million individuals.

LEGAL AND OPERATIONAL CHALLENGES

In January 2025, Israel introduced legislation prohibiting UNRWA's work within its territory and preventing official engagement with its staff. Nevertheless, the agency has continued its operations in Gaza and the West Bank, relying largely on Palestinian teams supported by a limited number of international staff.

Despite visa hurdles, funding shortages, and security threats, UNRWA's leadership has reaffirmed its commitment to remain and continue delivering aid.

Often described as the cornerstone of humanitarian support in Gaza, UNRWA's absence would likely result in the collapse of essential services. International donors play a critical role in sustaining its work — for instance, Ireland pledged €20 million in early 2025 to support programmes in health, food, and education.

Yet the agency's future remains fragile. More than 280 staff members have been killed, many facilities have been damaged, and financial uncertainty continues to threaten ongoing operations. Despite bans and mounting pressure, UNRWA still functions in Gaza, providing indispensable aid in increasingly dangerous and resource-limited conditions.

Other international agencies and NGOs — such as the International Committee of the Red Cross (ICRC), Médecins Sans Frontières (MSF), and local charities — fill gaps by providing medical aid, psychosocial support, and emergency shelter during escalations.

Still, aid is only a temporary patch on a long-term wound. Donors often face political and logistical barriers. Border crossings can close with little warning, delaying deliveries of medical supplies and food. Strict controls on dual-use goods — items that could be used for both civilian and military purposes, such as concrete and certain chemicals — mean that rebuilding destroyed infrastructure can take years.

International funding has also grown increasingly uncertain. Shifts in global politics, economic crises elsewhere, and donor fatigue have led to reductions in aid budgets. In recent years, UNRWA has faced major funding gaps, threatening its ability to provide services essential to daily life in Gaza.

HEALTH UNDER SIEGE: HOSPITALS ON THE BRINK

The healthcare system in Gaza illustrates the humanitarian crisis vividly. Chronic shortages of drugs and equipment leave hospitals constantly on edge. Treatments taken for granted elsewhere —

chemotherapy, kidney dialysis, complex surgeries — often depend on outside aid or patient referrals to hospitals beyond Gaza.

During escalations, hospitals become overwhelmed. Emergency rooms overflow with casualties, and vital medical supplies can run out within days. Doctors and nurses often work around the clock, sometimes without pay, driven by their commitment to their communities.

The blockade also affects training and professional development. Many medical professionals cannot leave Gaza to attend conferences or advanced training courses, limiting the growth of skills and knowledge critical for complex care.

EDUCATION INTERRUPTED

Education has long been a source of pride for Palestinian families, seen as a pathway to dignity and opportunity. Yet in Gaza, schools face repeated interruptions due to violence and infrastructure damage. Many school buildings serve double duty as emergency shelters during conflicts, leaving them damaged or overcrowded. UNRWA operates hundreds of schools, but class sizes often exceed 40–50 students, and resources are stretched thin.

Despite these challenges, literacy rates remain high. But a degree in Gaza too often fails to translate into employment, fuelling frustration among young people who feel trapped by circumstances beyond their control.

THE GLOBAL RESPONSE: EFFORTS AND LIMITATIONS

Internationally, the crisis in Gaza has drawn both urgent aid responses and prolonged diplomatic stalemates. Countries such as Qatar, Turkey, and several European donors have provided significant financial support for reconstruction, electricity, and humanitarian relief. UN agencies coordinate large-scale responses during escalations, from providing shelter to repairing water networks.

Yet there are enduring limits to what aid can achieve. Humanitarian assistance cannot substitute for political solutions. The blockade, combined with internal Palestinian divisions and recurring violence, keeps Gaza locked in a cycle where destruction outpaces rebuilding.

Efforts to broker longer-term ceasefires or reconstruction frameworks often stall over disagreements between Israel, Palestinian factions, and regional actors. The result is a piecemeal approach in which urgent needs are met, but root causes remain unaddressed.

THE CHALLENGE OF ACCESS AND NEUTRALITY

Humanitarian organisations face an added challenge: maintaining neutrality and access. In a context where all sides suspect foreign involvement, aid agencies must navigate political sensitivities carefully.

At times, restrictions have been imposed on aid organisations accused of indirectly supporting militant groups. Meanwhile, agencies have documented delays and denials when trying to bring in critical supplies labelled as dual-use.

The need for security vetting, combined with limited border openings, means that even when aid is available, getting it into Gaza remains unpredictable.

Living Conditions: The Day-to-Day Reality

For Gaza's residents, abstract debates translate into daily struggles:

- Power cuts force families to plan meals, laundry, and even medical treatments around electricity schedules.

- Shortages of clean water mean parents ration what they have for cooking and washing.

- High unemployment drives families into debt or leaves them dependent on relatives and charity.

- Frequent escalations force people to flee their homes at short notice — often more than once.

In such conditions, resilience is not a choice but a necessity. People adapt: using solar panels to power homes, recycling water, or teaching children at home when schools close.

Calls for Sustainable Solutions

Humanitarian groups stress that aid alone cannot resolve Gaza's crisis. Reports by the UN and international NGOs call for:

1. **Easing or lifting the blockade**: Allowing the flow of goods and people, while addressing legitimate security concerns through monitored mechanisms.

2. **Political reconciliation among Palestinian factions**: Ending divisions that complicate governance and reconstruction.

3. **Sustainable development**: Moving beyond emergency aid to foster economic growth, job creation, and infrastructure rebuilding.

4. **Protection of civilians**: All parties must uphold international humanitarian law.

Without these steps, Gaza risks further deterioration. The cycle of destruction and reconstruction will continue.

A HUMANITARIAN CRISIS WITH A HUMAN FACE

At its core, Gaza's crisis is about people: parents trying to protect children, students clinging to education as a lifeline, doctors saving lives under impossible conditions. It is about millions trapped between political paralysis, economic isolation, and recurring violence.

While the international community responds with aid, the crisis persists because its roots are as much political as material. Lasting change will require bold diplomacy, respect for human rights, and the political will to address the deeper causes of the conflict.

Until then, Gaza's residents live with profound uncertainty — enduring hardship with remarkable resilience, but still waiting for a peace that remains out of reach.

AID IN GAZA

Targeting of Humanitarian Workers and the Collapse of Protection

The Gaza Strip — long subject to blockade, bombardment, and political manipulation — stands as one of the starkest examples of a humanitarian crisis born of protracted conflict and deliberate policy. For civilians, aid is not a luxury but a lifeline. Yet the act of delivering that aid, and the people who risk their lives to do so, have become targets in a conflict where the space for neutrality and humanitarian protection has collapsed.

Medical staff, aid workers, and journalists in Gaza are no longer treated as impartial actors but as enemies — a perception that has cost many their lives. Beyond the immediate danger, this targeting threatens the survival of a population already living on the edge.

This chapter explores how aid in Gaza has become politicised, why humanitarian workers are being killed, and what this reveals about the erosion of international humanitarian norms.

A LIFELINE ENTANGLED IN CONFLICT

Humanitarian aid in Gaza includes emergency medical services, trauma care, food distribution, water and sanitation projects, and the rebuilding of homes and schools destroyed by repeated military assaults. These efforts should be protected under international law as strictly neutral and life-saving. But in Gaza, aid work cannot be separated from politics: decades of occupation, blockade, and recurrent military operations shape every effort.

The blockade, imposed by Israel since 2007 and enforced to varying degrees by Egypt, controls almost every aspect of Gaza's economy and daily life. It restricts imports of medical equipment, construction materials, and even basic supplies under the claim of potential "dual use". The result: chronic shortages, crumbling infrastructure, and a health system unable to cope with mass casualty events.

FROM NEUTRAL ACTORS TO SUSPECTED THREATS

Under international law, humanitarian workers are meant to operate neutrally and impartially, serving civilians regardless of politics. In Gaza, these principles have been steadily eroded.

Israeli authorities often portray aid workers, medical staff, and even international NGOs as suspect — sometimes accused, without evidence, of collaborating with Hamas or covering militant activity. These claims, echoed publicly and diplomatically, fuel an atmosphere of suspicion that compromises both the safety of aid workers and the willingness of governments and donors to support humanitarian programmes.

For civilians, the result is devastating: delays, funding cuts, and fewer services at the very moment when needs are greatest.

DISPROPORTIONATE VIOLENCE AND ITS VICTIMS

Over the years, attacks have targeted hospitals, ambulances, UN schools used as shelters, and aid convoys have all been attacked. Medical personnel and journalists have been killed, even when clearly identified by vests or markings.

Israeli officials often argue that Hamas embeds itself within civilian areas, turning hospitals and schools into "legitimate targets". Local medical staff, international NGOs, and human rights groups challenge this narrative, documenting facts on the ground.

Yes, Gaza is densely populated, and fighters may operate among civilians. But this does not cancel the obligation under international law to distinguish between civilians and combatants and to protect humanitarian workers.

Even if fighters are nearby, attacks must be proportionate and targeted, not blanket strikes on civilian infrastructure. The widespread destruction witnessed in Gaza — entire residential neighbourhoods levelled, hospitals repeatedly hit, aid convoys attacked — raises serious doubts that this standard is not being upheld.

WHY SO MANY AID WORKERS AND MEDICAL STAFF HAVE BEEN KILLED?

The killing of aid workers and medical staff in Gaza are not just accidents or the consequence of "fog of war". Several factors contribute to these casualties:

1. Systematic targeting and intimidation

Rather than being treated as neutral, humanitarian staff are cast as collaborators with militants. This framing, repeated in public statements and media, creates an environment where attacks on them become politically acceptable — even tacitly sanctioned.

2. Blockade and denial of access

The blockade itself acts as collective punishment, limiting the entry of supplies, fuel, and equipment. Ambulances have been prevented from crossing checkpoints; patients needing urgent treatment outside Gaza have been denied permits. These policies systematically undermine the delivery of aid and emergency medical services.

3. Urban density and disregard for proportionality

Gaza's population density makes civilian harm likely in any military action. But the sheer scale of bombardment, often described by witnesses as indiscriminate or disproportionate, has produced mass casualties, including aid workers.

4. Silencing of witnesses

Journalists, human rights monitors, and medical staff who document violations also face intimidation, arrests, or worse. Their deaths or disappearances silence testimony and evidence crucial for accountability.

HUMANITARIAN CONSEQUENCES

The impact of this violence and obstruction goes far beyond the tragic loss of individual lives:

- **Collapse of healthcare**: Repeated strikes on hospitals and clinics have pushed Gaza's health system to the brink. Patients go untreated, lifesaving surgeries are delayed or impossible, and essential medicines run out.

- **Loss of skilled personnel**: Experienced doctors, nurses, and aid workers are killed or forced to flee. Training replacements takes years — time Gaza does not have.

- **Psychological trauma**: Constant danger and grief erode the mental health of humanitarian staff, many of whom are themselves displaced or mourning relatives.

- **Erosion of neutrality**: Once humanitarian workers are portrayed as enemies, they lose access to the communities most in need, deepening suffering.

- **Weakening accountability**: Without witnesses, documenting violations becomes harder, allowing abuses to continue with impunity.

INTERNATIONAL LAWS: A PROMISE NOT KEPT

The Geneva Conventions and customary international law provide clear protections for medical staff, humanitarian workers, and journalists in conflict zones. Attacks on them are not only immoral; they are grave breaches that may amount to war crimes.

Yet enforcement remains limited. Investigations are blocked, perpetrators rarely face justice, and geopolitical interests shield Israel from meaningful consequences. Civilians in Gaza pay the price.

CHALLENGING OFFICIAL NARRATIVES

Israel repeatedly claims that Hamas uses hospitals, schools, and UN facilities as military sites. Human rights monitors argue that these claims lack sufficient, credible evidence to justify the scale and frequency of attacks. International law requires proof through thorough investigation, not sweeping assertions.

Even if fighters are present, humanitarian law demands proportionality and discrimination — attacks must avoid civilians and protected facilities. Strikes that kill doctors treating the wounded, bomb shelters housing displaced families, or destroy water and sanitation systems clearly breach these rules.

THE ROLE OF THE INTERNATIONAL COMMUNITY AND DONORS

International silence — or muted diplomatic criticism — has enabled the killing of aid workers and the destruction of Gaza's civilian infrastructure. Some governments have even cut funding to humanitarian agencies on the basis of politically motivated accusations rather than verified evidence.

Instead, there should be stronger support for:

- **Independent investigations**: Free access for UN agencies, human rights monitors, and journalists to document attacks and verify claims.

- **Humanitarian corridors**: Guaranteed safe passage for aid convoys, ambulances, and evacuations.

- **Legal accountability**: Use of international mechanisms to investigate and prosecute grave violations.

- **Protection of neutrality**: Rejection of rhetoric that frames aid workers as enemies.

Depoliticising Aid: What Must Change

For aid to remain life-saving, it must be free from political obstruction. This requires:

- **Respect for humanitarian principles**: Recognising aid workers and medical staff as neutral actors.

- **Ending collective punishment**: Lifting the blockade that punishes all civilians for the actions of armed groups.

- **Separation of military and civilian spaces**: Armed groups should avoid placing fighters near civilian facilities, but allegations must be substantiated, not assumed.

- **International pressure**: States with influence must demand respect for international law, not provide diplomatic cover for violations.

The Shrinking Space for Humanity

In Gaza, the targeting and demonisation of humanitarian workers reflects a wider assault on the principles meant to protect civilians in war. When aid workers, doctors, and journalists are killed, it is not only a tragedy for their families — it is an attack on the idea that even in war, humanity must prevail.

These are not accidents, nor can vague security claims justify them. They reflect policy choices that place military objectives and political control above civilian life.

Humanitarian aid is not political by nature, but it has been politicised by those who see it as a threat rather than a duty. Restoring protection for aid workers, ensuring accountability for violations, and upholding international law are not optional. They are the only way to protect the millions who rely on aid for survival — and to defend the principle that human life must never be reduced to a bargaining chip in conflict.

A CATALOGUE OF HORROR

Human Rights Violations and Suffering

The Gaza Strip, a densely populated coastal enclave home to over two million Palestinians, has long been a focal point of conflict and humanitarian distress. The latest eruption of violence has left behind a staggering toll of human suffering, devastation, and violations of fundamental human rights. As bombs fell and families were displaced, the world watched a humanitarian catastrophe unfold—a grim reminder of the brutal costs of war. This chapter catalogues the harrowing realities of the conflict: the injuries sustained, the violations committed, and the desperate plight of Gaza's civilians.

MASSIVE CIVILIAN CASUALTIES AND INJURIES

One of the most devastating aspects of the conflict has been the staggering number of civilian casualties. Hospitals and health organisations on the ground report thousands of deaths, with a significant proportion being women, children, and elderly civilians. Unlike combatants who wear uniforms and operate on battlefields, Gaza's civilians are trapped in a densely packed urban environment, making the distinction between military and civilian targets tragically blurred.

The injuries sustained by survivors are often severe and life-altering. Bombardments have caused traumatic amputations, burns, shrapnel wounds, and severe head injuries. Hospitals, already crippled by years of blockade and repeated assaults, are overwhelmed. Medical facilities frequently run out of essential supplies such as blood, anaesthesia, and antibiotics. The shortage of electricity disrupts life-saving medical procedures and the operation of critical equipment, such as ventilators.

Mental health consequences are also profound. Children living through constant bombardment suffer from severe psychological trauma, including post-traumatic stress disorder (PTSD), anxiety, and depression. The destruction of schools and the displacement of families add layers of insecurity and uncertainty about the future.

DESTRUCTION OF CIVILIAN INFRASTRUCTURE

Beyond human casualties, the conflict has ravaged Gaza's infrastructure. Entire neighbourhoods have been reduced to rubble by airstrikes and artillery shelling. Residential buildings, markets, mosques, and schools have been targeted or damaged, displacing tens of thousands of families.

Electricity and water infrastructure have also been heavily damaged. Power cuts, sometimes lasting 20 hours or more daily, have become routine, affecting hospitals, water pumping stations, and sanitation facilities. The destruction of water infrastructure has led to contaminated drinking water, thereby increasing the risk of outbreaks of waterborne diseases, such as cholera.

Hospitals and clinics themselves have been struck or forced to close due to the bombardment, compounding the medical crisis. The destruction of roads and bridges has hindered the delivery of humanitarian aid and the evacuation of the wounded.

BLOCKADE AND HUMANITARIAN CRISIS

Gaza has been under a land, sea, and air blockade for over 18 years, severely restricting the movement of people and goods. This blockade has crippled the economy and basic services long before the recent conflict erupted.

During the latest war, the blockade has been intensified, cutting off fuel, food, medical supplies, and construction materials vital for rebuilding. Humanitarian agencies have repeatedly warned of a catastrophic shortage of essentials. The blockade prevents Gazans from seeking medical treatment outside the Strip, trapping the wounded and sick in dire conditions.

Food insecurity has soared, with many families unable to access sufficient or nutritious food. Malnutrition risks rise sharply, especially among children. The blockade, combined with the destruction caused by the war, has plunged Gaza deeper into a humanitarian abyss.

HUMAN RIGHTS VIOLATIONS

Numerous reports from human rights organisations have catalogued serious violations committed during the conflict by the Israeli Defence Forces (IDF), with particular concern over disproportionate and indiscriminate attacks on civilians in Gaza.

International humanitarian law prohibits targeting civilians and mandates the protection of non-combatants. However, in Gaza, airstrikes have hit densely populated residential areas, medical facilities, and shelters. These attacks have been described as disproportionate and indiscriminate, and they constitute war crimes. Human rights groups have also documented the use of explosive weapons with wide-area effects in populated areas, further endangering civilians.

Additionally, there have been credible allegations of forced displacement within Gaza, where families are pressured to evacuate their homes without safe alternatives, compounding their vulnerability.

THE IMPACT ON CHILDREN

Children are among the most vulnerable victims of this conflict. Reports indicate that thousands of children have been killed or injured. Schools, where children should find refuge and education, have been destroyed or repurposed as shelters, often targeted by airstrikes.

The psychological trauma faced by children growing up amid violence is incalculable. Many suffer nightmares, anxiety, and fear for their safety and future. The disruption to education also affects their long-term prospects, risking a lost generation.

The United Nations and child protection agencies have emphasised the urgent need for child-centred humanitarian responses, including mental health support, safe schooling, and protection from recruitment by armed groups.

THE HEALTH SYSTEM ON THE BRINK OF COLLAPSE

Gaza's health system has been stretched beyond breaking point. Repeated conflicts, the blockade, and damage to infrastructure have left hospitals understaffed, undersupplied, and overwhelmed.

During the war, many hospitals have faced power outages, shortages of oxygen, and a lack of essential medicines. Medical staff are working under extreme pressure, often without adequate protective equipment. The risks to health workers are significant, and some have been injured or killed in attacks.

The health system's collapse threatens not only those injured in the conflict but also patients needing routine care, including pregnant women, chronic disease sufferers, and children needing vaccinations.

THE PSYCHOLOGICAL TOLL AND LONG-TERM CONSEQUENCES

Beyond immediate physical injuries and infrastructure damage, the war inflicts deep psychological scars on Gaza's population. Years of blockade, poverty, and repeated violence have created a pervasive sense of despair.

The trauma of losing family members, homes, and community support systems fuels cycles of grief and anger. Mental health services are scarce, and stigma often prevents those affected from seeking help.

The long-term consequences of war also include economic devastation, loss of livelihoods, and increased poverty, which in turn exacerbate health and social challenges.

INTERNATIONAL RESPONSE AND CHALLENGES

International humanitarian organisations have mobilised to provide aid, but their efforts face significant obstacles. Access to Gaza remains tightly controlled, and humanitarian supplies are often delayed or blocked.

The security situation complicates aid delivery, and damaged infrastructure hinders logistics. Fuel shortages limit the operation of hospitals, water treatment plants, and humanitarian vehicles.

The international community has condemned attacks on civilians and called for ceasefires, but a durable peace remains elusive. Political deadlock and regional tensions continue to fuel the cycle of violence.

CALLS FOR ACCOUNTABILITY AND JUSTICE

Human rights organisations, UN bodies, and activists have called for impartial investigations into alleged violations of international law. Accountability is seen as essential to ending impunity and preventing future atrocities.

However, political complexities and a lack of enforcement mechanisms have often stalled meaningful justice. The lack of media access to Gaza further complicates the gathering and documentation of evidence.

CONCLUSION

The war on Gaza has wrought immense suffering, leaving scars that will last for generations. The catalogue of horrors—civilian casualties, injuries, destruction of infrastructure, humanitarian crises, and human rights violations—is a stark testament to the catastrophic cost of armed conflict on vulnerable populations.

For the people of Gaza, the path ahead is fraught with challenges: rebuilding homes, healing wounds, and reclaiming a sense of normalcy amid uncertainty. The international community must prioritise humanitarian aid, insist on the protection of civilians, and support efforts toward a just and lasting peace.

Above all, the stories of those who have suffered must not be silenced. Bearing witness to their pain and resilience is a crucial step toward a future where such horrors are no longer repeated.

RESISTANCE, REFUGEES, AND THE RUBBLE

Gaza's Struggle for Survival

In the heart of Gaza City, where towers once scraped the sky, now stand only shattered walls and powdery grey dust. The air smells of rotting flesh and burning plastic; the soundtrack is the hum of drones overhead, punctuated by distant booms. Yet amid the ruins, people move with quiet determination: cooking over makeshift stoves, teaching children in tent schools, writing poetry on the ruins.

Gaza's story isn't just one of destruction. It is also a story of survival: of refugees holding onto dignity for generations; of resistance that is political, cultural, and spiritual as much as military; of a people determined not to vanish, no matter how many times the bombs fall. This is the story of Gaza's struggle for survival — from the first tents in 1948 to today's tents under fresh ruins.

THE MAKING OF A REFUGEE STRIP

Gaza's journey into crisis began long before today's war. In 1948, more than 700,000 Palestinians were expelled or fled from what became Israel — an event known to Palestinians as the Nakba, or "catastrophe." Around 200,000 ended up in Gaza, whose population at the time was barely 80,000.

They lived in tents, then concrete-block refugee camps. They were promised the right to return — a right recognised by UN Resolution 194 — but decades passed, and the tents became crowded alleys of concrete and corrugated metal. Today, around 80% of Gaza's 2.3 million residents are refugees or their descendants. The memory of lost villages remains alive in family stories, embroidered dresses, and hand-painted signs.

OCCUPATION AND BLOCKADE

In 1967, Israel occupied Gaza during the Six-Day War. Settlements were built; the military ruled daily life. In 2005, Israel withdrew settlers but kept control of Gaza's airspace, coastline, and most border crossings. Israel, with Egypt, imposed a blockade after Hamas won elections in 2006.

For nearly two decades, Gaza has been described by many observers — including UN officials — as an "open-air prison." Movement is tightly restricted; most residents have never left. The blockade has crushed the economy. Unemployment hovers around 50%, higher for youth. Water is mostly undrinkable; electricity comes only for a few hours a day. Yet life — somehow — goes on: weddings, football matches, university graduations, street markets.

RESISTANCE BEYOND ROCKETS

When the word "resistance" is mentioned, most imagine armed fighters and rocket launches. But resistance in Gaza is also a grandmother telling stories so that children remember their villages; students learning despite bombed schools; and farmers tending to olives by the fence.

Cultural resistance is everywhere: hip-hop in refugee camps, paintings on broken walls, plays performed in the ruins of theatres. Writers like Refaat Alareer, killed in an Israeli strike in December 2023, turned poetry into defiance. As Alareer wrote, "If I must die, let it bring hope

/ let it be a tale retold." Even joy itself can be resistance — a refusal to be reduced to victims.

CYCLES OF DESTRUCTION

Since the blockade began, Gaza has endured repeated wars: 2008–9, 2012, 2014, 2021, and now the devastating campaign. Each time, the cycle repeats: bombardment, civilian casualties, shattered infrastructure, then partial reconstruction — often halted by new violence.

Each war deepens trauma, but also deepens resolve. A man in Khan Younis, standing beside rubble, told a reporter: *"We have no choice but to rebuild. Where else can we go?"*

Children born under siege and war know no life without drones overhead. Psychologists warn of mass PTSD. Yet many youth volunteer to teach younger kids or distribute food — turning suffering into solidarity.

DISPLACEMENT WITHIN DISPLACEMENT

October 2023 brought displacement on an unimaginable scale. Israel ordered the residents of northern Gaza to evacuate south. Entire neighbourhoods emptied overnight. But nowhere proved safe: Israel struck Rafah, Khan Younis, and even designated "safe zones."

Families fled multiple times. UN shelters, built for hundreds, housed thousands. Disease spread; food and clean water ran out. By mid-2024, over 1.9 million people were displaced — some living again in tents, like their grandparents in 1948. For many, the symbolism is bitter: the Nakba repeated in new form.

THE POLITICS OF SURVIVAL

Gaza's struggle isn't only humanitarian; it is political. Residents often say: "We don't want just aid. We want rights." Hamas, which won elections in 2006, rules Gaza but is deeply controversial among Palestinians. Some see it as a legitimate resistance movement; others blame it for authoritarianism and decisions that brought disaster. But even Hamas's critics often say the root problem isn't internal politics, but the blockade and occupation.

The Palestinian Authority, which governs parts of the West Bank, is viewed by many in Gaza as distant and ineffective. Meanwhile, negotiations for peace have collapsed; new settlements rise in the West Bank. Gaza, trapped and battered, becomes both symbol and pawn in a wider struggle over Palestine's future.

LIVING UNDER SIEGE

Daily life in Gaza requires ingenuity. Fishermen risk gunboats to bring back meagre catches; farmers coax crops from salt-poisoned soil. Engineers build homemade solar systems; students study by phone light.

Internet blackouts during bombings cut Gazans off from the world — but neighbours spread news by word of mouth. In cafes and homes, debates swirl: why is the world silent? Will there ever be peace? A university student named Abeer said, "We are tired, but we still dream. Maybe not for us — but for our children."

INTERNATIONAL RESPONSE: TOO LITTLE, TOO LATE

UN agencies warn of famine. Hospitals, many destroyed, struggle without medicine. Aid convoys are blocked or bombed. Humanitarian workers themselves are killed. Western governments issue statements urging "restraint," yet continue arms sales to Israel. Protesters worldwide march under slogans like "Ceasefire now" and "Stop arming genocide," but diplomatic pressure remains limited.

Some countries, led by South Africa, bring legal cases accusing Israel of genocide. The ICJ orders Israel to stop killing civilians and allow aid — orders Israel disputes or ignores. For Gaza's people, these actions feel slow and distant compared to the immediacy of missiles.

REBUILDING — AND REMEMBERING

After every war, Gazans rebuild: homes, schools, dreams. Reconstruction materials, restricted by the blockade, arrive slowly or not at all. Many families rebuild on the same spot, knowing it might be bombed again.

Memory plays a central role. Families keep keys from homes lost in 1948; children learn village names they've never seen. Poets and artists document each war, so history isn't written only by the powerful. As one writer said, "Even if they destroy our houses, they cannot destroy our memory."

THE HUMAN COST

Beyond numbers — tens of thousands killed, many of them children — are countless private tragedies: a girl who lost her leg and still smiles; a father searching for his child under rubble; a doctor forced to choose which patient to save. Yet hope persists, stubborn as olive trees. People still fall in love, still write songs, still plant flowers beside tents.

A QUESTION OF JUSTICE

Gaza's struggle for survival isn't just physical. It is also a fight against erasure: the fear that suffering will be normalised, resistance labelled terrorism, and the right to live freely forgotten.

International law promises protection for civilians, the right to return for refugees, and accountability for war crimes. Yet enforcement is scarce. Many Gazans feel a sense of international sympathy, but little concrete justice. A Palestinian journalist summed it up, "We don't need pity; we need freedom."

THE FUTURE: UNCERTAIN, BUT UNBROKEN

What comes next? Another fragile ceasefire? Continued siege? A political settlement? Many fear worse violence. Yet many also dream: of open borders, of rebuilding, of children growing up without fear.

Gaza's survival so far isn't guaranteed by treaties or armies, but by the daily courage of ordinary people: teachers holding class in ruins; mothers cooking bread over wood fires; youth writing poems that cross the digital siege. They know tomorrow may bring more bombs — yet refuse to give up.

BEYOND HEADLINES

For much of the world, Gaza appears on TV during wars, then disappears. But for those inside, it is home: a place of grief and joy, destruction and creativity, despair and resilience. In the end, Gaza's story isn't only about war. It is about people who, despite everything, still declare: "We are here. We will not be erased." Their struggle for survival continues — in the rubble, in the refugee camps, in every act of daily resistance. And until justice comes, their defiance itself remains a powerful form of hope.

Youth and Education in Gaza

Life Interrupted by War

To grow up in Gaza is to come of age under blockade, amid ruins that are rebuilt only to be destroyed again. For young people here, education is both a lifeline and a battleground — not only because of the physical risks to schools and students, but because it carries the weight of hope in a place where the future is too often stolen by war.

This chapter delves into how the conflict has disrupted education in Gaza, shaped the aspirations and mental health of its youth, and challenged a society that still clings fiercely to learning as a form of resistance and dignity.

A Generation under Siege

Nearly half of Gaza's population — around one million people — are under the age of 18. They are children and teenagers who have known nothing but life under blockade, and who have lived through multiple military escalations.

For them, education is more than just schooling. It represents stability, identity, and an act of defiance against the circumstances that surround them. Yet it is also constantly under threat: schools become shelters during bombardments, classrooms turn into ruins, and academic years are repeatedly interrupted.

Even between escalations, the reality of daily life under blockade — shortages of electricity, limited materials, and psychological stress — undermines the very foundations of education.

SCHOOLS IN THE CROSSFIRE

Gaza has more than 700 schools, many run by the United Nations Relief and Works Agency (UNRWA), which serves Palestinian refugees who make up the majority of the population.

During conflicts, schools often become shelters for families fleeing bombardment. While this is vital for saving lives, it also leaves schools damaged and delays the return to classes. After major escalations, the sight of shattered desks, scorched blackboards, and broken windows is tragically common.

The 2014 war, for example, destroyed or damaged over 250 schools. In subsequent escalations — including those in May 2021 and October 2023 — dozens more were affected, and rebuilding takes months or years, with funding often uncertain and complicated by restrictions on importing construction materials.

Even when buildings are intact, overcrowding is severe. Many schools operate double or even triple shifts, meaning children attend for only a few hours each day. Classrooms often hold 40–50 students, making personalised teaching almost impossible.

THE PSYCHOLOGICAL TOLL

Beyond the physical damage, war leaves invisible wounds. The constant fear of violence — hearing drones overhead, airstrikes nearby, or mourning classmates — shapes how children learn and see the world.

Psychologists in Gaza report widespread trauma among students: anxiety, nightmares, aggression, and difficulties concentrating. A

2022 study found that over 80% of children in Gaza showed signs of emotional distress. Teachers describe classrooms where children jump at loud noises or draw pictures filled with tanks, planes, and blood.

The blockade itself adds to this burden. Many young people have never left Gaza, creating a sense of isolation. The walls around them literally and figuratively limit their horizon.

UNRWA and NGOs provide psychosocial support, but the scale of need far exceeds resources. Teachers, often themselves traumatised, try to create safe spaces, but the recurrence of violence makes healing difficult.

INTERRUPTED DREAMS

In Gaza, education is highly valued and culturally revered. Families celebrate exam results with pride; degrees are seen as passports to dignity. Yet the conflict and blockade have turned that promise into uncertainty.

University students face disrupted semesters when campuses close during conflicts. Graduates, even those with top marks, encounter staggering unemployment rates — often over 60% among young people. Many young men and women invest years in study, only to see few opportunities at the end.

For aspiring doctors, engineers, and scientists, pursuing specialised studies abroad is almost impossible. Getting an exit permit through the Erez crossing into Israel or the Rafah crossing into Egypt is complicated and sometimes impossible, especially during periods of heightened tension.

Those who do leave often face a painful choice: return to Gaza and limited prospects, or stay abroad, separated from family indefinitely.

GIRLS' EDUCATION: PERSEVERANCE AMID HARDSHIP

Girls in Gaza generally have high enrolment rates in school, and female students often outperform their male peers academically. Yet conflict and poverty create specific challenges.

Families struggling economically may prioritise sons' education or push daughters into early marriage. During escalations, safety concerns can keep girls at home longer than boys.

Despite these obstacles, young women in Gaza have become symbols of resilience. Many pursue university degrees in medicine, law, or technology, challenging social norms and economic hardship. They view education not just as personal advancement, but as a way to contribute to rebuilding society.

TEACHERS ON THE FRONTLINES

Educators in Gaza are more than instructors; they are often counsellors, community leaders, and first responders in times of crisis. Teaching under blockade presents daily challenges: frequent power cuts, shortages of paper and teaching aids, and large class sizes. Teachers must adapt lessons to unpredictable schedules, switching between morning, afternoon, and evening shifts.

During escalations, some teachers continue classes remotely — over WhatsApp messages or radio broadcasts — trying to maintain a sense of continuity. After conflicts, they help children process trauma, even as they cope with their own losses. Many teachers have suffered damage to their homes or lost family members. Yet they return to classrooms, driven by a commitment to students and a belief in education as a form of resistance.

UNIVERSITIES UNDER PRESSURE

Higher education in Gaza is well-developed, with several universities offering degrees in fields such as engineering, medicine, and law. But these institutions face severe constraints. Blockade restrictions limit access to lab equipment, books, and online services. Faculty exchanges, conferences, and research collaborations are difficult because travel permits are hard to obtain.

Even when online learning is possible, power cuts and slow internet connections disrupt classes. Students must plan study sessions around unpredictable electricity schedules.

Despite this, Gaza's universities have produced accomplished graduates. Many have gained international recognition for research and innovation, a testament to determination overcoming structural barriers.

INNOVATION AND ADAPTATION

Necessity has fostered creativity among Gaza's youth and educators. Some examples include:

- **Solar-powered classrooms**: Reducing reliance on unreliable electricity grids.

- **Online learning initiatives**: Local NGOs and universities are creating digital resources accessible even during closures.

- **Psychosocial education**: Incorporating trauma awareness into teacher training and curricula.

- **Youth entrepreneurship**: Programmes teaching coding, design, and small business skills to prepare students for freelance work and digital markets.

These efforts do not solve the root problems, but they show how young people and educators adapt under extreme constraints.

THE BROADER IMPACT ON SOCIETY

Education is not only about individual opportunity; it shapes the fabric of society. In Gaza, interrupted schooling has implications for public health, economic development, and social cohesion.

High unemployment among educated youth fuels frustration and, for some, hopelessness. It also contributes to migration pressures, as those who can leave often do.

Conversely, education remains one of the few pillars holding society together. Schools and universities serve as community centres, safe spaces, and symbols of normalcy amid chaos.

AID AND SUPPORT: A LIFELINE, NOT A SOLUTION

International agencies, including UNRWA, UNICEF, and numerous NGOs, play a critical role in sustaining education in Gaza. They provide school supplies, rebuild damaged classrooms, fund psychosocial programmes, and train teachers.

Yet these efforts face chronic funding shortfalls. Political changes among donor countries, economic crises in other regions, and shifting global priorities have led to budget cuts. UNRWA in particular has faced existential funding crises, threatening services for hundreds of thousands of students.

Humanitarian aid keeps education going, but it cannot substitute for structural change, which includes ending the blockade, achieving political reconciliation, and addressing the root causes of conflict.

HOPE AND RESILIENCE

Despite everything, hope persists. Graduation ceremonies are moments of joy; children still dream of becoming doctors, engineers, poets, and teachers. Parents invest what little they have in books and uniforms, seeing education as a legacy worth any sacrifice.

Students organise reading clubs, volunteer for community projects, and create art that expresses both pain and aspiration. Their resilience is not born of choice but of necessity, yet it speaks to an enduring belief: that education can break cycles of despair.

A FUTURE WORTH FIGHTING FOR

In Gaza, education is not merely preparation for the future; it is an act of survival in the present. It is how a generation interrupted by war clings to the idea that tomorrow can be different.

For Gaza's youth, the classroom is a refuge from violence, a place where imagination can flourish beyond the concrete walls of the blockade. For teachers, it is a front line of a different kind, where they fight to keep hope alive.

Yet hope alone is not enough. Without addressing the structural injustices that disrupt learning — blockade, conflict, and occupation — Gaza's students will continue to see their dreams deferred.

The world owes these young people not just sympathy, but action: to protect schools, support teachers, and insist on their right to learn free from fear because in the end, the future of Gaza and of peace itself rests in the minds and hearts of its youngest generation. And no child's education should ever be interrupted by war.

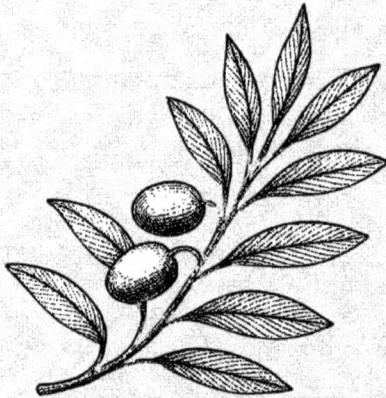

PART-II
LEGAL, MORAL, AND POLITICAL QUESTIONS

GENOCIDE OR SELF-DEFENCE?

Testing Israel's War Against Gaza Under International Law

In a crowded courtroom at The Hague in January 2024, lawyers for South Africa faced a panel of judges from the International Court of Justice (ICJ). Their accusation was direct and historic: Israel, they argued, is committing genocide against the Palestinian people in Gaza. Across the aisle, Israel's legal team rejected the charge as "baseless and grotesque", defending its military campaign as a lawful exercise of self-defence.

This moment crystallised a question that has haunted the modern era: when does self-defence become aggression, and when does aggression become genocide?

As Gaza's ruins multiply and the civilian death toll soars past 70,000, this question isn't only legal — it is moral, political, and deeply human.

THE LEGAL LANDSCAPE: SELF-DEFENCE AND ITS LIMITS

The right to self-defence is enshrined in Article 51 of the UN Charter: "Nothing in the present Charter shall impair the inherent right of individual or collective self-defence if an armed attack occurs." Israel's government cites this right as justification for its operations in Gaza, describing them as necessary responses to Hamas' attack on October 7, 2023, which killed around 1,200 Israelis and involved hostage-taking and atrocities.

But international law draws boundaries. Even in self-defence, military actions must meet two core principles: proportionality and distinction.

- Proportionality: Force used must not be excessive in relation to the concrete and direct military advantage anticipated.

- Distinction: Parties must distinguish between combatants and civilians; attacks directed at civilians are strictly prohibited.

The reality in Gaza, where entire residential areas have been reduced to rubble, medical infrastructure targeted, and civilian casualties overwhelmingly outnumber combatant deaths, raises grave questions about these principles.

DEFINING GENOCIDE

Under the 1948 Genocide Convention, genocide means acts committed with the intent to destroy, in whole or in part, a national, ethnic, racial, or religious group. These acts include killing members of the group, causing serious bodily or mental harm, and deliberately inflicting conditions calculated to bring about its destruction.

It isn't only the scale of killing that defines genocide, but the specific intent to destroy a group as such. Proving intent is notoriously difficult — it is rarely openly confessed. But courts can infer intent from patterns of action and statements by leaders.

In Gaza, UN experts, legal scholars, and human rights organisations argue that Israel's campaign — massive civilian killings, forced displacement, and targeting of essential life systems — combined with statements by Israeli officials describing Palestinians as "human animals" or vowing to "flatten Gaza", points to genocidal intent.

The ICJ case: South Africa vs Israel

In late 2023, South Africa filed a case at the ICJ accusing Israel of violating the Genocide Convention. South Africa's lawyers presented evidence: thousands of civilian deaths, widespread destruction of homes, water and electricity systems deliberately targeted, and statements by Israeli leaders that frame the entire population as enemies.

In January 2024, the ICJ issued provisional measures, ordering Israel to prevent genocidal acts and report back regularly, while not ruling yet on the merits of the case. By May, further evidence of starvation and continued bombing had sharpened global concern.

Israel argues its campaign targets Hamas, not the Palestinian people, and blames civilian casualties on Hamas' alleged tactic of embedding fighters in civilian areas. Israeli officials frame the war as existential, describing Hamas as an "ISIS-like enemy".

The question of proportionality

After October 7, Israel launched an air and ground campaign unprecedented in Gaza's history. Whole city blocks were destroyed within hours. Satellite imagery shows nearly half of Gaza's buildings damaged or destroyed. Reports from UN agencies describe deliberate targeting of hospitals, schools, and even refugee camps.

Israel's defence rests on proportionality, arguing that Hamas' attack was so severe that the military response, while tragic, is justified.

However, proportionality doesn't weigh the total number of civilians killed; it compares the anticipated military advantage of each strike to the harm to civilians. Dropping 2,000-pound bombs in densely populated areas, knowing civilians will die, is difficult to square with this principle.

As legal scholar Eyal Benvenisti observes, "Even a legitimate war goal cannot justify means that kill thousands of civilians for marginal military gains."

DISTINCTION: COMBATANTS VS CIVILIANS

Hamas is a political-military organisation that sometimes blends into civilian areas. But international law requires attackers to make every feasible effort to verify that targets are military. Civilian objects — like hospitals, schools, and residential towers — cannot be targeted unless used for military purposes, and even then, the harm to civilians must not be excessive.

Reports from Human Rights Watch, Amnesty International, and UN agencies detail repeated strikes on clearly civilian infrastructure without evidence of military use.

The Israeli army says it warns civilians before strikes—through leaflets, calls, or "roof-knocking". Critics argue these warnings are inadequate in a territory where people have nowhere safe to go. Who in their right mind would believe that Gazans ignore such warnings and remain where bombs are about to fall? It just doesn't add up.

FORCIBLE DISPLACEMENT AND STARVATION

One element of genocide is deliberately inflicting conditions calculated to destroy the group. Since October, more than 1.9 million Gazans — 85% of the population — have been displaced, many multiple times. Safe zones promised by Israel have been bombed. Aid convoys have been blocked or attacked. Famine now threatens northern Gaza, according to the World Food Programme.

Starvation as a method of war is explicitly prohibited under international humanitarian law. Blocking water, food, and fuel isn't merely a military tactic; it can constitute a war crime — and, if intended to destroy a group, part of genocide.

INTENT: WORDS AND DEEDS

In legal terms, proving genocidal intent is the hardest threshold. But in the Gaza case, words from Israeli leaders have raised alarms:

- Defence Minister Yoav Gallant: "We are fighting human animals... Gaza will not return to what it was."

- President Isaac Herzog: "It's an entire nation out there that is responsible."

- Other officials spoke of making Gaza "disappear", "erasing" cities, or forcing population transfers to Sinai.

Courts have historically used such statements, combined with large-scale killing and destruction, to infer intent.

DOUBLE STANDARDS AND POLITICAL SHIELDS

International law is meant to apply equally. But powerful states shape enforcement. The US, UK, and EU states have continued to supply Israel with weapons and diplomatic cover, even as evidence of atrocities mounts.

When Russia bombed Mariupol, Western leaders called it a war crime. When Israel bombs Rafah, they urge "restraint.". The law doesn't change — but politics shields some violators and condemns others.

South Africa's ICJ case aims to bypass this political shield, appealing to the universal language of law.

VOICES FROM THE GROUND

Legal arguments can feel abstract. In Gaza, the reality is immediate: numerous children shot in the head by snipers, children pulled from rubble, hospitals overflowing, and entire families wiped out.

Mohammed, a doctor in Gaza City, described in a voice message: "Every day we receive dozens of bodies. Some are unrecognisable — burnt or crushed. We have no words left."

For survivors, the debate over genocide isn't about semantics; it is about whether the world sees them as human — and whether their deaths matter.

THE ROAD TO ACCOUNTABILITY

The ICJ case could take years. Meanwhile, the International Criminal Court (ICC) is also investigating war crimes by all parties. Its prosecutor, Karim Khan, announced in May 2024 that he seeks arrest warrants for senior Israeli and Hamas leaders.

Israel, like the US, is not a member of the ICC and rejects its jurisdiction. But arrest warrants could limit travel and sharpen diplomatic pressure. The big question is which country would arrest Benjamin Netanyahu?

Human rights lawyers also pursue universal jurisdiction cases in national courts — a reminder that impunity isn't guaranteed.

CAN GENOCIDE CHARGES STOP A WAR?

Legal processes are slow; bombs fall fast. Yet history shows that naming crimes can change political dynamics. The ICJ's provisional ruling emboldened protest movements and increased the diplomatic isolation of Israel. Some arms shipments were suspended by European states after court findings. Legal accountability alone won't end the violence — but it makes complicity harder.

BEYOND LAW: THE MORAL QUESTION

Ultimately, the debate isn't only about legal thresholds. It is about whose lives are protected by law and whose deaths are tolerated.

If a state can bomb a besieged civilian population, displace millions, and block aid, all while claiming self-defence, then the promise of "never again" following the Holocaust becomes hollow. The Genocide Convention was created to prevent mass destruction, not to justify it.

WATCHING HISTORY UNFOLD

The question "genocide or self-defence" will echo in courts, parliaments, and protests for years. But in Gaza, the answer feels clear to those living under the bombs. As one survivor said, "They call it war. We call it *the* destruction of our people." History will judge not only what happened, but how the world responded when the law's promise clashed with the power of the state.

Israel's Devastation of Gaza

The Inescapable Verdict of Genocide and War Crimes

For more than a year now, the Gaza Strip has borne the brunt of an unrelenting military assault that has devastated its people and infrastructure beyond measure. Reports from Gaza's Ministry of Health and international humanitarian agencies reveal a staggering death toll exceeding 70,000 Palestinians. Tens of thousands more lie injured, many with permanent disabilities. Amid this catastrophic loss of life, over two million people remain trapped in a strip of land crippled by an ironclad blockade that denies them basic necessities such as food, clean water, medicine, and electricity.

Entire neighbourhoods lie in ruins, hospitals and clinics have been bombed repeatedly or are barely functioning due to a lack of fuel and electricity, and countless families have been wiped out in their homes. Yet, this human tragedy is far more than the collateral damage of war.

Legal experts and human rights advocates argue with increasing urgency that the scale, intensity, and intent behind Israel's military campaign in Gaza constitute not only war crimes but also genocide under international law. This is not a conclusion drawn lightly or from political bias but from a rigorous analysis of international treaties, decades of judicial precedent, and the overwhelming facts on the ground.

The term 'genocide' carries immense weight. It was coined to describe the gravest crime against humanity—the intentional destruction of an entire group of people. According to the 1948 Genocide Convention, genocide involves acts committed with the purpose of destroying, wholly or in part, a national, ethnic, racial, or religious group. This destruction can take many forms: killing members of the group, inflicting serious bodily or mental harm, deliberately creating living conditions intended to bring about physical destruction, imposing measures to prevent births, or forcibly transferring children to another group. Among these, the crucial and defining element is the intent to annihilate the group as such.

When we look at Gaza today, the grim reality aligns closely with these legal criteria. The human toll alone is staggering. Over 70,000 Palestinians, mostly civilians, including a devastating number of children, have been killed during this ongoing campaign. The humanitarian situation is nothing short of catastrophic. Hospitals that once served millions now operate in near total darkness, lacking fuel for generators and running out of essential medicines. Clean water is scarce as aquifers are destroyed or contaminated. Food shortages are widespread, and fuel deprivation has grounded ambulances and emergency services, compounding the suffering.

International law recognises that deliberately inflicting such conditions—starvation, medical deprivation, and destruction of essential infrastructure—can amount to genocide. In Gaza, these conditions have not occurred incidentally or as an unavoidable side effect of combat; rather, they have been imposed deliberately and systematically.

This is evident not only in the physical devastation but also in the repeated public declarations from Israeli political and military officials. Statements that openly call for Gaza to be "flattened," describe the population as "human animals," and vow to prevent their recovery for decades clearly signal an intent to destroy not just military targets but the people themselves.

Proving intent is notoriously difficult in law, but international courts have long accepted official statements and consistent policy patterns as decisive evidence. The parallels to past genocides are stark. In the 2007 Bosnia v. Serbia case, the International Court of Justice confirmed that targeting part of a protected group with the aim of destroying it qualifies as genocide. The population of Gaza—millions of Palestinians living in a tightly confined area—has been subjected to this targeting on an unprecedented scale. The International Criminal Tribunal for the former Yugoslavia's 2001 conviction of Radislav Krstić for genocide in Srebrenica similarly emphasised how intent could be inferred from the combination of mass killing and official rhetoric. The International Criminal Tribunal for Rwanda's 1998 Akayesu judgement further established that imposing deadly living conditions, including starvation and denial of medical care, meets the criteria for genocide.

Even setting aside the charge of genocide, Israel's conduct in Gaza unquestionably constitutes war crimes. International humanitarian law strictly prohibits the intentional targeting of civilians and civilian infrastructure. It forbids the use of starvation as a method of warfare and outlaws collective punishment of entire populations. The ongoing siege of Gaza, cutting off food, water, fuel, and medical supplies, fits precisely this description. The International Court of Justice's 2004 advisory opinion reaffirmed the illegality of collective punishment under international law, a principle flagrantly violated by the blockade.

Predictably, Israel and its supporters argue that this military campaign is a lawful act of self-defence against Hamas militants who operate within densely populated civilian areas. However, international law makes it clear that violations committed by one party do not justify breaches by the other. The 1997 judgement of the International Criminal Tribunal for the former Yugoslavia in the Tadić case clarified that all parties in a conflict must protect civilians and uphold the principles of proportionality and distinction. The presence of militants among civilians cannot excuse the widespread and disproportionate destruction inflicted on Gaza's entire population.

Nor do the violent and incendiary statements from Israeli leaders constitute mere rhetoric—they have been recognised in multiple legal precedents as evidence of genocidal intent when paired with corresponding actions.

In response to the mounting evidence and international pressure, the International Court of Justice has issued provisional measures ordering Israel to prevent genocidal acts and to allow unimpeded humanitarian aid into Gaza. The International Criminal Court has opened investigations into war crimes and crimes against humanity committed in the region. While justice may be slow and imperfect, these actions represent essential steps toward holding perpetrators accountable and upholding the rule of law.

The facts are undeniable: tens of thousands dead, a civilian population subjected to systematic starvation and deprivation, infrastructure destroyed on a massive scale, and public statements revealing an intent to destroy. The only legally and morally consistent conclusion is that Israel's military campaign in Gaza constitutes genocide and war crimes. To deny or minimise this reality is to ignore the law, the evidence, and the suffering of millions.

But this is not just a legal issue — it is profoundly human. Survivors of the conflict recount the horrors of losing loved ones, of children dying for lack of medicine or fuel to run life-saving equipment. They tell stories of entire families buried beneath the rubble of their homes. Doctors describe working in hospitals without electricity and running out of basic supplies while patients succumb to preventable causes. These voices are the living testimony behind the cold legal terms.

The international community faces a historic moral and legal imperative. Upholding justice for Gaza is not optional; it is essential to preserving the very foundations of international law and human dignity. If the world turns away from this injustice, it risks normalising impunity for the most egregious crimes against humanity. The consequences will extend far beyond Gaza, threatening vulnerable populations everywhere.

In sum, the evidence and law converge on one inescapable truth: Israel's campaign in Gaza is genocide and war crimes. The global community must act—through enforceable measures, through justice, and through unwavering solidarity with the victims. Anything less is a betrayal of humanity itself.

HUMAN SHIELDS AND HUMAN COSTS

Myths and Realities of Urban Warfare in Gaza

Since the latest war on Gaza began, Israeli officials have repeatedly invoked the same justification for high civilian casualties: Hamas, they claim, "uses civilians as human shields." The phrase has become a staple of press conferences, social media posts, and diplomatic briefings. It is invoked to explain the bombing of apartment blocks, refugee camps, and even schools and hospitals.

But behind this narrative lies a deeper story: how modern urban warfare really works, what international law actually says, and, most importantly, what this framing costs — in civilian lives, in truth, and in prospects for accountability.

THE POWER OF A PHRASE

The concept of "human shields" is emotionally potent: it conjures an image of armed fighters hiding behind women and children. It reframes mass civilian deaths not as tragic errors, but as someone else's crime.

Israel's Prime Minister, Benjamin Netanyahu, has said, "Hamas is responsible for every civilian casualty because it hides behind civilians." Similar statements echo across Western media, often unchallenged. The logic is simple: if civilians die, blame the enemy for putting them at risk. Yet human rights lawyers, military analysts, and even some Israeli veterans say this logic is often dangerously simplistic — and, in Gaza, deeply misleading.

International humanitarian law (IHL), including the Geneva Conventions and Additional Protocol I, prohibits two things:

- Using civilians to "shield" military objectives from attack.

- Launching indiscriminate or disproportionate attacks, even if the enemy hides among civilians.

In other words, even if an armed group illegally embeds itself in a civilian area, the attacking force must still take precautions: choose weapons carefully, verify targets, and cancel or suspend strikes that would cause excessive harm to civilians relative to the expected military advantage. As Adil Haque, a professor of international law, explains, "The presence of human shields doesn't give a free pass to bomb densely populated areas without discrimination."

URBAN WARFARE — AN UNAVOIDABLE REALITY?

Gaza is a narrow strip of land, roughly twice the size of Washington, D.C., but home to over 2 million people. Cities like Gaza City and Khan Younis are packed with apartment blocks, markets, mosques, and hospitals. About 80% of residents are refugees living in cramped camps.

For any local armed group — whether Hamas or other factions — hiding in the desert isn't an option: there is no desert. Gaza is almost entirely urban.

former Israeli soldiers from the group Breaking the Silence have acknowledged this reality. One veteran said, "When you fight in Gaza, you fight where people live. That doesn't automatically mean the enemy is using them as human shields."

Israeli officials cite examples: rocket launchers near schools, tunnels under civilian areas, and command centres allegedly in hospitals. Very few of these claims have been documented by journalists, and UN reports state that claims of this nature not only remain unverified but are vehemently denied by medics and aid workers.

Hamas, for its part, has built tunnels under Gaza—a fact it openly admits, calling them "tunnels of resistance". Some tunnels reportedly run beneath civilian areas. But building tunnels in an urban zone is not, by itself, the same as forcing civilians to stand in harm's way.

True "human shielding" under international law requires deliberate coercion: compelling civilians to remain in, or move to, military sites to deter attack. The evidence for this — especially systematic coercion — is far scarcer than the rhetoric suggests.

FROM LAW TO PROPAGANDA

The "human shields" claim has become a powerful rhetorical weapon. It:

- Shifts moral and legal responsibility away from the attacker.

- Justifies high civilian death tolls to domestic and international audiences.

- Pre-empts criticism from human rights groups.

A similar narrative has been used elsewhere. In the 2016 battle for Mosul, Iraqi and U.S. officials blamed ISIS's use of civilians to explain deadly airstrikes. In Afghanistan, NATO forces often invoked "human shields" to justify strikes that killed civilians.

The key danger, say critics, is that this framing can normalise civilian deaths — turning them from avoidable tragedies into inevitable facts of war.

PROPORTIONALITY AND DISTINCTION

Under IHL, the core principles are:

- Distinction: attacks must target only military objectives.

- Proportionality: expected civilian harm must not be excessive in relation to the concrete military advantage.

Even if the enemy hides among civilians, these rules remain in force. Yet in Gaza, entire neighbourhoods have been reduced to rubble. The UN reports thousands of children killed and hospitals, bakeries, and water plants destroyed. Israel often says these were "Hamas sites". But proportionality is a legal calculation, not a slogan — and it must weigh each strike individually.

Human Rights Watch and Amnesty International argue that many Israeli attacks are "disproportionate" or "indiscriminate", violating IHL regardless of Hamas's conduct.

WHO IS A CIVILIAN?

In asymmetric warfare, the line between civilian and combatant is blurred by design — but legally, the definition remains clear. A 16-

year-old boy carrying bread to his family is a civilian. A nurse treating wounded fighters is still a civilian, unless she directly participates in hostilities. Yet the "human shields" narrative can recast whole populations as legitimate targets — especially in political discourse, if not strictly in law.

Some Israeli ministers have openly called for collective punishment. Heritage Minister Amichai Eliyahu, for example, suggested using a nuclear bomb on Gaza — statements that, while shocking, reflect an undercurrent: the idea that civilian status is conditional, and civilians are guilty by association.

CALLS TO EVACUATE — AND THEIR LIMITS

Israel often defends strikes by saying it warns civilians to flee via leaflets, phone calls, or text messages. Legally, advance warning is required "unless circumstances do not permit." However, warnings must be "effective" — offering civilians a genuine opportunity to escape. In Gaza, residents say warnings often direct them to areas that are later bombed or to overcrowded shelters without food or water. Many people cannot move, including the elderly, disabled individuals, and hospital patients. Telling civilians to flee does not nullify their protected status. Nor does it erase the proportionality requirement.

THE HUMAN COST — BEYOND NUMBERS

Statistics — 70,000 killed (by mid-2025), 70% women and children — can feel abstract. But behind them are stories:

- A family in Jabalia camp was crushed under rubble after a night strike; rescuers pulled out children alive, but missing limbs.

91

- Doctors performing amputations without anaesthesia because medicine ran out.

- Journalists killed while filming, wearing clearly marked press vests.

For these victims, debates about "human shields" don't change the loss.

DOUBLE VICTIMS

If Hamas did, in fact, compel civilians to remain near military targets, those civilians would become double victims: used illegally by one side and then killed or wounded by the other.

But proving such coercion is difficult. In many cases, civilians stay because they have nowhere else to go — or because the entire territory is under attack.

ACCOUNTABILITY: A MISSING PIECE

International courts rarely prosecute violations of proportionality or unlawful targeting. The ICC opened an investigation into alleged war crimes in Palestine in 2021, but it remains incomplete. Israel argues it conducts internal investigations. Critics call these slow and opaque and rarely lead to indictments. Without credible accountability, the law risks becoming rhetoric — invoked to justify violence rather than restrain it.

Beyond Gaza: a global pattern

The "human shields" narrative isn't unique to Israel–Gaza. It appears whenever states or armies face non-state actors in urban spaces:

- Russia in Chechnya accused rebels of hiding among civilians.

- The Syrian regime called opposition-held towns "terrorist nests".

- Saudi Arabia labelled Yemeni civilians in Houthi areas as human shields.

In each case, high civilian casualties followed.

The moral hazard

The biggest danger, experts warn, is moral hazard: if armies believe the enemy's presence among civilians justifies heavy bombing, they may bomb more, not less.

That risks transforming laws designed to protect civilians into justifications for harming them.

What could be done differently?

Military experts suggest:

- Strikes with smaller-yield weapons.

- Tighter intelligence verification.

- More accurate, real-time proportionality analysis.

- Greater transparency: publishing target lists and legal reasoning.

But political choices often override caution: speed of campaign, domestic pressure, or desire for deterrence.

TRUTH, LAW, AND HUMANITY

In modern warfare, particularly in asymmetric conflicts, both sides may violate the laws of war. But the existence of enemy violations does not legally — or morally — excuse one's own. When officials say, "They use human shields," it must not end the conversation. It should start a deeper question: even so, did you do everything possible to protect civilians? Were your attacks necessary, proportionate, and targeted?

For the people of Gaza, the debate is not abstract. It is measured in lives lost, limbs amputated, and children orphaned. And for the world, accepting "human shields" as a catch-all defence risks normalising what should remain unthinkable: mass civilian death as an acceptable price of war. Because once every bomb can be excused, the laws of war cease to protect anyone at all.

AMERICA'S COMPLICITY

How U.S. Foreign Policy Enables Atrocities in Gaza

For decades, U.S. foreign policy in the Middle East has been defined by a deep and often uncritical alliance with Israel. While couched in rhetoric about democracy and security, this partnership has, in practice, enabled the systematic oppression of Palestinians and, most recently, what many legal scholars and human rights organisations call genocide in Gaza. Through the steady flow of military aid, diplomatic cover at international forums, and a persistent refusal to hold Israel accountable, the United States has done more than stand idly by; it has actively supported policies that maim, displace, and kill civilians on a massive scale.

This chapter explores how American foreign policy has become complicit in the devastation unfolding in Gaza — and why this complicity is not a tragic accident, but a deliberate choice rooted in geopolitical calculations and a deeply flawed worldview.

A LONGSTANDING ALLIANCE BUILT ON MILITARY MIGHT

Since the late 1960s, Israel has been the largest cumulative recipient of U.S. foreign assistance. According to the Congressional Research Service, the United States has provided Israel with over $150 billion (adjusted for inflation), the vast majority of which is military aid. Today, Israel receives around $3.8 billion annually under a memorandum of understanding signed during the Obama administration.

This aid has helped Israel build one of the most advanced militaries in the world: fleets of F-16 and F-35 fighter jets, precision-guided munitions, missile defence systems, and state-of-the-art surveillance technologies. While American policymakers argue this assistance deters conflict and ensures Israel's security, the evidence from Gaza tells a darker story: these weapons are being used to demolish homes, hospitals, refugee camps, and entire neighbourhoods.

During the recent war, reports by human rights organisations, including Amnesty International and Human Rights Watch, have documented the use of American-made bombs and missiles in strikes that killed civilians and destroyed civilian infrastructure. These are not isolated incidents or unfortunate accidents; they are part of military operations that overwhelmingly target densely populated areas where civilians cannot escape.

DIPLOMATIC PROTECTION: SHIELDING ISRAEL FROM ACCOUNTABILITY

The United States' complicity extends beyond weapons. At international forums like the United Nations Security Council, successive U.S. administrations have used their veto power repeatedly to block resolutions calling for ceasefires, independent investigations into war crimes, and even basic humanitarian protection for Palestinian civilians.

For example, during some of the deadliest escalations in Gaza, the U.S. vetoed or watered down resolutions calling for immediate cessation of hostilities, despite mounting evidence of massive civilian casualties. This diplomatic shield enables Israel to continue military operations with impunity, knowing that meaningful international consequences are unlikely.

American officials justify these vetoes by citing Israel's right to self-defence, yet this right is not unlimited. International law requires proportionality and distinction between combatants and civilians. By blocking accountability mechanisms and undermining international law, the U.S. effectively gives a green light to violations, including attacks that independent observers describe as war crimes or acts of collective punishment.

THE GENOCIDE ACCUSATION: BEYOND RHETORIC

The charge of genocide is not made lightly. Under the Genocide Convention, genocide involves acts committed with the intent to destroy, in whole or in part, a national, ethnic, racial, or religious group. Legal scholars, UN experts, and prominent human rights lawyers argue that the scale and pattern of violence in Gaza—paired with dehumanising language from Israeli leaders and policies designed to make life unliveable—fit this definition.

Thousands of civilians, including a devastatingly high number of children, have been killed. Entire families have been wiped out. Basic necessities — food, water, electricity, and medical supplies — are systematically denied to over two million people. Hospitals and shelters have been bombed, and reconstruction is effectively impossible under the ongoing blockade.

On top of all of this, we have the suggestion by the American president (Trump) that the population be forcibly displaced, their homeland confiscated and turned into a holiday resort for the rich.

In this context, American military aid and diplomatic protection do not merely support Israel's security; they enable policies that legal scholars say meet the threshold of genocide. The U.S. cannot plausibly claim ignorance: reports from international agencies, media coverage, and even statements from its own allies document the devastating humanitarian impact. Yet aid continues to flow, and vetoes continue to block accountability.

THE HUMAN COST: FUNDING DEATH AND DESTRUCTION

When American policymakers debate military aid to Israel, the discussion often focuses on abstract questions of deterrence, regional stability, or shared democratic values. Rarely do they confront what this aid means on the ground.

It means American-made bombs flattening apartment blocks where entire families live. It means shells striking UN schools sheltering displaced civilians. It means U.S.-funded warplanes bombing hospitals, cutting off access to life-saving care. It means that every hour, children die not from unavoidable crossfire but from deliberate policies that starve and suffocate a trapped population.

This is not an inevitable byproduct of conflict; it is the direct result of choices made in Washington, where military support is treated as non-negotiable and civilian suffering as collateral damage.

Why does America do it? The strategic and political calculations

The question of why the U.S. maintains this posture despite global outrage has multiple answers, rooted in history, politics, and geopolitics.

1. Strategic alignment:

Since the Cold War, Israel has been seen as a key U.S. ally in a volatile region. American policymakers view it as a reliable partner that shares intelligence, helps counter Iran, and balances against adversaries.

2. Domestic politics:

The U.S. pro-Israel lobby, most prominently the American Israel Public Affairs Committee (AIPAC), wields significant influence in Congress. Criticising Israel has long been politically costly, with members of Congress facing fierce pushback, primary challenges, and donor pressure if they call for conditions on aid or criticise Israeli policies.

3. The war on terror paradigm:

Since 9/11, American foreign policy has framed conflicts through a counterterrorism lens, aligning itself with other states that claim to be fighting terrorism — even when those claims mask human rights abuses. Israel positions its military operations as necessary counterterrorism efforts, a framing that resonates in Washington.

4. A flawed moral narrative

American leaders often describe Israel as "the only democracy in the Middle East" and frame U.S. support as a defence of shared democratic values. This narrative ignores the reality of millions of Palestinians living under occupation and siege without basic rights.

VOICES OF RESISTANCE AND MORAL RECKONING

Despite bipartisan consensus in Washington, there is growing resistance. Some members of Congress, especially younger and more diverse lawmakers, openly criticise unconditional aid to Israel and call for accountability. Human rights organisations are increasingly vocal in condemning American complicity.

Among the American public, especially younger voters and minority communities, support for unconditional aid to Israel is waning. Protests have erupted across U.S. cities, demanding an end to military assistance and calling the war what many see it as: genocide.

Yet policy remains largely unchanged, revealing the disconnect between public opinion and political power.

BEYOND GAZA: BROADER MIDDLE EAST FAILURES

U.S. complicity in Gaza is part of a broader pattern in the Middle East, where American policy has often prioritised short-term stability, military alliances, and arms sales over human rights and long-term peace.

In Egypt, the U.S. supports a regime accused of widespread repression and human rights abuses. In Saudi Arabia, American weapons have fuelled a brutal war in Yemen, creating one of the world's worst humanitarian disasters. Across the region, democracy movements have been undermined or ignored when they threaten American strategic interests.

This approach has not delivered peace or security. Instead, it has fuelled cycles of violence, empowered authoritarianism, and deepened anti-American sentiment.

WHAT MUST CHANGE?

The crisis in Gaza demands more than expressions of concern; it demands a radical rethinking of U.S. foreign policy. This means:

- Ending unconditional military aid: Aid should be contingent on compliance with international law, human rights standards, and the protection of civilians.

- Supporting accountability: The U.S. should stop shielding Israel from investigations by international bodies and support credible enquiries into alleged war crimes.

- Centring human rights: American policy should be guided not by narrow strategic interests, but by the universal rights of all people — Israeli and Palestinian alike.

- **Addressing root causes:** Beyond emergency aid, the U.S. must push to end the blockade of Gaza, dismantle the occupation, and support genuine self-determination for Palestinians.

THE CHOICE AHEAD

America's complicity in the devastation of Gaza is not inevitable. It is the result of choices: to send weapons rather than withhold them, to protect an ally rather than protect civilians, to prioritise power over justice.

As bombs fall and bodies are buried, the U.S. faces a moral reckoning. It can continue to enable the killing of civilians under the banner of security — or it can choose a foreign policy rooted in human dignity and international law.

History will judge America not by its speeches about peace and democracy, but by its actions when confronted with the deliberate destruction of a trapped, occupied people. The time to choose differently is now.

DRAGGED INTO THE ABYSS

How Israel's Genocidal War on Gaza Is Revealing America's Moral Depravity

The United States of America is not suffering from a moral crisis—it is basking in one. Israel's genocidal campaign in Gaza is not tearing America's soul apart. It is exposing what lies at its core: a brutal, calculating indifference to human life when that life is Palestinian, Arab, Muslim, or inconvenient to its interests.

Over 70,000 Palestinians are dead. Gaza's cities lie in ruins. Hospitals have been reduced to piles of dust. Doctors have been executed in their operating rooms. Families buried under the rubble. Children burned, starved, dismembered. And the bombs that made this possible—the bombs that keep falling even now—are American. The funding is American. The diplomatic protection is American.

This is not passive complicity. This is active, deliberate participation in genocide. The United States is not standing by while horrors unfold—it is bankrolling them. It is providing the weapons, writing the cheques, vetoing the ceasefires, silencing the protests, and demonising the victims. There is no neutrality here. There is no misunderstanding. There is only raw, open-eyed depravity, broadcast live, and justified with the language of democracy and defence.

GENOCIDE WITH U.S. BRANDING

Gaza has become a graveyard for international law and human decency. Entire families have been eradicated. Tens of thousands of civilians—many of them children—have been slaughtered with impunity. Famine is being weaponised. Refugee camps are bombed in broad daylight. Journalists are executed. Humanitarian workers are targeted.

The United States has not only tolerated this, but it has also underwritten it. American-made bombs are dropped by Israeli jets over schools and hospitals. American taxpayer dollars fund the very munitions that tear through bodies and buildings. American vetoes at the United Nations are used to block even the faintest international rebuke.

This is not support for a defensive war. This is not an alliance. It is an unambiguous sponsorship of extermination. It is what happens when the political machinery goes unchecked—when American power is wielded not to prevent slaughter, but to guarantee it.

AMERICA – WHERE IS YOUR SOUL?

To suggest that this is "tearing America's soul apart" is to imply a rupture from moral ideals. But America is not deviating from its principles—it is executing them. This is the same country that obliterated Fallujah, that napalmed Vietnamese villages, and that supported juntas, coups, death squads, apartheid, and blockades wherever it served its interests. Gaza is not a break from America's tradition. It is its continuation.

This is not a crisis of identity—it is a confirmation of identity. America has always rationalised its atrocities through the language of security, civilisation, or God. It has consistently prioritised power over justice, profit over people, and domination over peace. What we are seeing in Gaza is not an exception—it is America, unmasked.

104

And yet, as Palestinians are crushed beneath concrete and starved behind barbed wire, there is a grotesque movement among some Americans to nominate Donald Trump for a Nobel Peace Prize. Let that sink in. In a time of genocide—one he helped embolden and architect—millions of Americans worship a man who represents the most vulgar expression of American imperial arrogance. Trump has openly talked about turning Gaza into a holiday resort, a playground for the wealthy. He is so depraved that he sees Gaza as real estate and thinks the forced dispossession and displacement of Palestinians is a good idea!

Donald Trump is not a peacemaker. He is not an honest broker. As president, he moved the U.S. embassy to Jerusalem in defiance of international consensus, gutted aid to Palestinian refugees, sanctioned the annexation of occupied territory, and proudly pushed the Abraham Accords—hollow agreements between Israel and Gulf dictatorships that bypassed Palestinians entirely. He empowered the worst elements of the Israeli far-right and dismissed Palestinian suffering as background noise.

To suggest that Trump deserves a peace prize is not just delusional—it is obscene. It is the logic of empire turned inward: to reward aggression, ethnic cleansing, and apartheid as long as they serve U.S. interests and flatter American egos. It is evidence that America has lost its moral compass—if it ever had one.

The Americans who cheer for Trump's faux diplomacy while Gaza is being levelled are not misinformed. They are indoctrinated, intoxicated by the delusion that domination equals peace and that colonised people must either submit or be erased. This is not ignorance. It is supremacist ideology, wrapped in the flag and blessed from evangelical pulpits.

EMPIRE'S MIRROR IMAGE

Israel functions as a mirror of the American Empire. It is a settler-colonial project, a fortress state built on the ruins of another people's homeland, justified through exceptionalism, sanctified by religious myth, and maintained through overwhelming violence. The United States supports Israel not in spite of these features—but because of them.

Let's be crystal clear: the notion of "justification through exceptionalism" refers to actions—no matter how extreme or oppressive—being defended by the belief that a particular country or group is inherently special, superior, or entitled to behave differently (often more harshly or aggressively) than others. In the context of Israel's policies, "justified through exceptionalism" refers to how Israeli leaders and many supporters argue that Israel's actions—such as military occupation, settlement expansion, and harsh measures against Palestinians—are acceptable or necessary because Israel sees itself as a unique, chosen, or exceptional nation with a special destiny or security concerns that outweigh normal international laws or human rights norms.

BIPARTISAN SUPPORT FOR GENOCIDE

Democrats and Republicans may squabble over budget ceilings and immigration policies, but they unite around the sanctity of Israeli militarism. Trump, Biden, and Obama all armed the occupation, shielded it diplomatically, and insulted the intelligence of the world by claiming "concern" while sending more weapons. This is not failure. This is policy.

And in the U.S. homeland, this depravity replicates itself. Students protesting genocide are arrested. Journalists are harassed. Faculty are blacklisted. Billionaires threaten universities. The pro-Israel lobby buys off Congress while the state criminalises solidarity through anti-BDS laws and smears of antisemitism. Gaza is not just a foreign warzone—it is a blueprint for domestic repression.

Anti-BDS laws passed by some governments—mostly in the United States—seek to punish or restrict support for the Boycott, Divestment, and Sanctions (BDS) movement against Israel. The BDS movement is a global campaign that calls for various forms of boycott against Israel until it complies with international law, ends the occupation of Palestinian territories, grants equal rights to Palestinian citizens of Israel, and recognises Palestinian refugees' right of return.

Anti-BDS laws typically do things like:

- Prohibit state contracts with companies or individuals that support BDS.

- Bar public institutions from doing business with entities that boycott Israel.

- Penalise organisations or individuals who participate in BDS activities.

Critics argue these laws violate free speech rights by criminalising or economically punishing peaceful political protest and advocacy.

Supporters claim they protect Israel from economic harm and combat what they call antisemitism. The right-thinking world is sick of the antisemitism trump card being played whenever Israel is criticised for its criminal actions.

In short, anti-BDS laws are designed to legally counteract and suppress the BDS movement, limiting people's ability to boycott Israel as a form of political expression.

NO MORE ILLUSIONS

To suggest that America is losing its way is to lie. The U.S. is not sleepwalking into catastrophe. It is marching proudly into it, flags waving, arms deals signed, and lies polished for prime-time consumption.

Internationally, the consequences are already severe. In the Global South, American hypocrisy is now a joke—bitter, dangerous, and deadly. In Europe, long-time allies are breaking ranks, recognising Palestine and condemning U.S. obstructionism. In the Muslim world, America's image is in ruins. Among young people in the U.S. itself, there is a rising tide of fury, disgust, and disillusionment.

This generation does not want excuses. It wants accountability. It does not want platitudes about democracy—it wants an end to genocide. And the state is responding not with dialogue, but with riot police, mass arrests, and censorship. America's mask is slipping, revealing the terrible truth about so-called American democracy.

A Choice—But Not for Long

There is still, theoretically, time to change course. But that window is narrowing. To begin reversing this descent, the United States would have to immediately end all military aid to Israel. Not delay. Not a condition. End. It would need to support international legal investigations into war crimes—no exceptions. It would need to publicly declassify intelligence, admit complicity, and take diplomatic and economic steps to hold Israel accountable.

At home, it would need to repeal laws criminalising Palestinian solidarity. Restore academic freedom. Protect protest. End the persecution of dissent. And beyond that, it would have to confront the ideological disease at the heart of this empire: the belief that some lives matter more than others.

But let's be honest: none of this is likely to happen without mass pressure and moral revolt. The political establishment has shown itself to be too compromised, too cowardly and too depraved. And so the burden falls to the people—to speak, to resist, to name genocide as genocide, and to never again mistake silence for neutrality.

History Is Watching

The ultimate judgement will not come from politicians, pundits, or PR campaigns—it will come from history itself and from the collective conscience of humanity. When future generations look back on this era, they will see a United States that chose convenience over courage, that bartered its proclaimed values for bombs and vetoes. They will see a nation that elevated a genocidal regime to the status of untouchable ally and that silenced its own people's cries for justice with propaganda and repression. They will see a country that allowed entire communities—mothers, children, elderly—to be erased and then looked away.

This is not a legacy to be proud of. This is a stain on the soul of any country that calls itself free and just. The American people must confront this reality—not as a distant abstraction, but as a moral imperative. To remain silent, to accept these atrocities as collateral damage in geopolitical games, is to become complicit in the bloodshed.

If America cannot stand up and demand an immediate end to the slaughter, if it cannot dismantle the systems that enable this genocide, then it has abandoned the very principles that once made it a beacon of hope. The time for equivocation has passed. This moment demands radical clarity, unflinching truth, and relentless action.

Because the lives extinguished in Gaza are not just numbers on a screen—they are a human indictment of every handshake that seals a weapons deal, every diplomatic shield that blocks justice, and every voice that refuses to speak out.

EUROPE'S DEAFENING SILENCE

The EU's Failure to Condemn Israel's War Crimes in Gaza

When war tears through Gaza, leaving tens of thousands dead and entire neighbourhoods reduced to rubble, one might expect the European Union—a global champion of human rights and international law—to lead the chorus of condemnation. Yet, amid the unfolding humanitarian catastrophe and mounting allegations of war crimes, the EU's response has been strikingly muted, cautious, and often complicit in its silence.

This silence isn't accidental. It reflects a troubling pattern of political calculus, strategic interests, and institutional paralysis that undermines Europe's professed values and leaves Gaza's victims bereft of powerful allies in the international arena.

THE HUMAN TOLL: A CRISIS IGNORED

As of mid-2025, more than 70,000 Palestinians have been killed in Gaza since the latest Israeli military offensive began. The United Nations reports that about 70% of the casualties are women and children. The densely populated Gaza Strip, home to over 2 million people, has become a landscape of ruin. Hospitals lie in ruins, schools have been shelled, and over a million Gazans have been displaced from their homes.

Despite these grim facts, the European Union's official statements have been measured, almost diplomatic to a fault. Calls for "restraint" and "de-escalation" pepper official communications, but explicit references to Israel's disproportionate use of force, the destruction of civilian infrastructure, or accusations of war crimes are conspicuously absent. This muted response contrasts sharply with the scale of the humanitarian crisis unfolding on the ground.

This ambivalence is not new. The EU's record on Israel-Palestine over decades reveals a consistent reluctance to challenge Israel directly, even when credible reports implicate it in breaches of international law.

In 2014, during the Gaza war that killed over 2,200 Palestinians, the EU's statements heavily balanced condemnation of rocket attacks from Gaza with calls for restraint on both sides. In 2021, as violence surged again, EU leaders expressed "concern" but stopped short of strong condemnations or calls for accountability.

Today, as evidence mounts of possible war crimes—including deliberate targeting of civilian sites, use of excessive force, and a blockade amounting to collective punishment—the EU's official posture remains cautious. It has neither called for independent investigations nor unequivocally condemned Israel's conduct. This is in stark contrast to its vociferous condemnation of Russia for its invasion of Ukraine and its willingness to finance Ukrainian resistance. This pattern of cautious statements about Israel's brutal campaign of genocide in Gaza is a symptom of deeper structural and political challenges within the EU.

POLITICAL AND ECONOMIC INTERESTS AT PLAY

The European Union's relationship with Israel is complex and multifaceted. Israel is a significant trading partner, a technology and innovation hub, and a strategic ally in a turbulent Middle East region. Many EU member states rely on Israel for intelligence sharing, counterterrorism cooperation, and regional stability efforts.

Economic ties further complicate the EU's ability to take a firm stand. Israel and the EU have a comprehensive trade agreement dating back to 1995, and their economic relationship has grown steadily over the years. This interdependence creates political incentives to avoid confrontation that could jeopardise trade, technology exchange, or security partnerships.

Moreover, internal EU politics present an obstacle. Member states vary widely in their approaches to Israel-Palestine, reflecting their own histories, political constituencies, and foreign policy priorities. Countries like Germany and Hungary have maintained particularly close political and military ties with Israel, whereas Ireland has been outspoken in condemning Israel's blatant breaches of international and humanitarian law. The political influence of pro-Israel lobbying groups within some EU countries further complicates efforts to build consensus for strong action.

Given the EU's decision-making processes, which often require consensus or broad agreement, these internal divisions tend to produce cautious, lowest-common-denominator statements that fail to address the severity of the situation adequately.

HUMAN RIGHTS VS. REALPOLITIK

The EU's foundational treaties emphasise respect for human rights, democracy, and the rule of law. The EU prides itself on being a normative power, promoting these values globally. However, in practice, realpolitik often takes precedence over principles.

European Commission President Ursula von der Leyen has called for "a lasting ceasefire", and EU High Representative Josep Borrell has referred to the "tragic situation", but neither has explicitly condemned Israel's military actions in Gaza or labelled them potential war crimes.

This cautious diplomatic language sends a dangerous signal: it tacitly permits the normalisation of civilian suffering and legal impunity, undermining the EU's credibility on human rights and international law.

LEGAL OBLIGATIONS AND MISSED OPPORTUNITIES

The EU is not just a political entity; it has legal responsibilities under international law. It has repeatedly emphasised its commitment to international humanitarian law (IHL), human rights treaties, and the UN Charter. The Rome Statute, which established the International Criminal Court (ICC), defines war crimes, including targeting civilians and disproportionate attacks — allegations increasingly raised against Israel's Gaza operations.

The ICC launched an investigation into alleged war crimes in Palestine in 2021, focusing on both Israeli and Palestinian actions. The EU has publicly supported the ICC's role globally and funds human rights monitoring in conflict zones. Yet, when it comes to Israel-Palestine, the EU has not championed this investigation robustly. It has avoided pressuring Israel to cooperate fully or condemning efforts to undermine accountability.

Moreover, the EU's humanitarian aid to Gaza, though vital, is insufficient on its own. Providing aid addresses the symptoms of conflict but not the root causes or questions of justice and accountability.

THE COST OF SILENCE

Europe's reluctance to condemn Israel carries profound consequences. For Palestinians, it means a lack of meaningful international protection or redress. Without pressure from powerful actors like the EU, Israel's military campaigns face little external deterrence, emboldening further violations.

For international law, the EU's silence weakens the enforcement of norms designed to protect civilians and hold perpetrators accountable. When war crimes are ignored by major powers, the norms risk erosion, inviting more violence in the future.

For Europe itself, this stance undermines its moral standing and influence on the world stage. The EU's identity as a defender of human rights is compromised, which in turn affects its capacity to influence other global crises effectively and alienates millions of European citizens who demand principled foreign policy.

Finally, the failure to confront violations head-on deepens the cycle of violence and mistrust, making a peaceful and just resolution more distant than ever.

VOICES OF CRITICISM WITHIN EUROPE

Criticism of the EU's approach has grown louder in recent months. Prominent human rights organisations operating within Europe, including Amnesty International and Human Rights Watch, have condemned the EU's cautious language as complicity by omission. They highlight the urgent need for the EU to break its pattern of diplomatic hedging and demand accountability.

Several Members of the European Parliament (MEPs) have voiced their frustration, calling for urgent and unequivocal condemnations of Israeli actions, as well as the suspension or review of EU-Israel trade agreements until human rights are respected.

Civil society campaigns, protests, and petitions across major European cities have pressured EU institutions to adopt firmer stances, yet progress remains slow and limited.

LESSONS FROM HISTORY

Europe's failure to respond decisively to past atrocities—whether in Rwanda, Bosnia, or Syria—serves as a sobering reminder of the cost of silence.

International justice mechanisms like the ICC depend on the political will of key actors, such as the EU. When that political will is lacking, impunity flourishes, victims are denied justice, and atrocities become more frequent.

If the EU fails to act decisively now, history may judge it harshly for turning a blind eye to one of the gravest humanitarian crises of our time.

WHAT MUST CHANGE?

The European Union stands at a critical juncture. To reclaim its moral authority and play a meaningful role in ending the violence and addressing justice in Gaza, the EU must:

- Issue clear, unequivocal condemnations of all violations of international law, including Israel's disproportionate military actions and the targeting of civilians in Gaza.

- Support independent and impartial investigations into alleged war crimes and ensure accountability mechanisms are enforced, including backing the ICC's work and calling on Israel to cooperate fully.

- Suspend or rigorously review trade and cooperation agreements with Israel, ensuring they do not facilitate or reward violations of human rights and international law.

- Apply diplomatic pressure on all parties to respect ceasefires, end the blockade, and allow unrestricted humanitarian access.

- Amplify Palestinian voices, including humanitarian actors, civil society organisations, and human rights defenders, ensuring their perspectives shape EU policy.

- Increase humanitarian aid and reconstruction assistance while coupling it with robust political advocacy that addresses root causes of the conflict.

CONCLUSION

The European Union stands at a crossroads. Will it continue to hide behind cautious language and political expediency, or will it embrace its role as a defender of human rights, international law, and justice?

The devastation in Gaza demands more than expressions of concern. It demands clear action, principled leadership, and accountability.

Europe's silence is deafening — and its consequences are devastating. The world is watching. The victims of Gaza deserve no less than a Europe that stands firmly on the side of justice, humanity, and peace.

GERMANY'S MORAL COLLAPSE

Complicity in the Gaza Genocide

As the world watches the systematic destruction of Gaza, where entire families are buried under rubble and vital infrastructure is obliterated, Germany continues to wrap its silence—and complicity—in the rhetoric of "historical responsibility". But the lessons of history demand 'never again' for anyone, not just one people. Instead, Germany has chosen to supply weapons, criminalise protest, muzzle dissent, and offer Israel unconditional support, even in the face of credible allegations of genocide. This is not moral leadership; it is moral failure.

In this chapter, we expose the depth of Germany's complicity in the atrocities unfolding in Gaza, tracing its dimensions across arms exports, economic entanglements, diplomatic manoeuvring, and political repression. Germany's posture is not only deeply hypocritical — it's dangerous.

FROM RESPONSIBILITY TO REPRESSION: THE HISTORICAL GUILT NARRATIVE

Post-World War II Germany rightly took on the burden of responsibility for the Holocaust — a genocide committed in the heart of Europe by a modern, industrialised state. The memory of the Nazi extermination of six million Jews has shaped modern German identity, foreign policy, and public discourse. This collective guilt was institutionalised — taught in schools, memorialised in architecture, and woven into the nation's legal and diplomatic commitments.

But over time, this genuine historical reckoning has been selectively repurposed to serve an entirely different agenda: unconditional support for the State of Israel, regardless of its actions. What began as an effort to ensure "Never Again" has, in practice, evolved into a dogma that brooks no nuance — where any criticism of Israeli policy is viewed as a slippery slope back to antisemitism.

This intense national sensitivity has stifled open debate, suppressed criticism, and created a climate where solidarity with Palestinians is equated with Holocaust denial or hatred of Jews. Holocaust memory is no longer a tool for universal justice — it has become a political shield that allows the German state to ignore or justify Israel's apartheid, occupation, and even possible genocide.

In doing so, Germany is not healing from its past — it is repeating the structural logic of it, not in word, but in the wilful abandonment of another oppressed people. Historical guilt must never become a licence for new injustices.

Arming the Occupation: Germany's Military Support for Israel

Germany is one of Israel's top arms suppliers. Between 2008 and 2022, Germany delivered more than €1.6 billion worth of military equipment to Israel, including naval submarines, patrol boats, surveillance systems, and small arms. Crucially, many of these weapons are not symbolic; they are deployed directly in the occupation and repeated assaults on Gaza.

Germany has supplied Israel with Dolphin-class submarines capable of launching nuclear missiles, and in 2023–2024 alone, Berlin approved dozens of new export licenses even after thousands of Palestinian civilians had already been killed. The government insisted there was "no evidence" that the exported weapons were being used to commit violations of international law — a wilfully blind claim that stands in sharp contrast to the visible realities of Gaza's destruction.

By continuing arms exports during an ongoing and widely condemned military campaign, Germany is in clear violation of its obligations under both EU and international law — including the Arms Trade Treaty, which prohibits exports when there is a risk they may be used to commit war crimes or crimes against humanity.

ECONOMIC COLLABORATION AND TRADE TIES

Beyond arms, Germany and Israel maintain deep economic ties in defence, tech, and cyber-surveillance. German-Israeli research collaborations include technologies used in both civilian and military contexts — including facial recognition, AI surveillance, and urban control technologies deployed in the West Bank and East Jerusalem.

German firms—particularly those in the defence and security sectors—have joint ventures or subcontracting deals with Israeli arms manufacturers such as Elbit Systems, known for producing drones and munitions used in Gaza. These partnerships are often funded or encouraged by public institutions like the Fraunhofer Society, under the guise of "innovation" and "security".

Germany is also Israel's largest European trading partner and continues to engage in free trade agreements that include products

121

made in illegal settlements in the occupied territories. The European Court of Justice ruled in 2019 that such products must be labelled accordingly, but enforcement in Germany is negligible.

DIPLOMATIC HYPOCRISY: SHIELDING ISRAEL, UNDERMINING INTERNATIONAL LAW

Germany presents itself as a global champion of the rules-based international order. Yet when it comes to Israel, it does everything in its power to obstruct those very rules. When South Africa filed a genocide case against Israel at the International Court of Justice (ICJ) in early 2024, Germany did not just decline to support it—it actively opposed the case.

The German Foreign Ministry declared it "baseless", despite overwhelming evidence presented by UN experts, journalists, and humanitarian organisations on the ground in Gaza.

Berlin even took the extraordinary step of intervening legally on Israel's behalf in the ICJ proceedings, attempting to block accountability through procedural manoeuvring. This is not neutrality — it is an attempt to prevent justice. And it confirms that Germany, while lecturing others about law and order, is willing to undermine international courts if the defendant is Israel.

Germany's complicity is not limited to the realm of diplomacy and defence. It has also taken the dangerous route of criminalising domestic opposition to Israel's war on Gaza.

Pro-Palestinian demonstrations have been repeatedly banned or violently dispersed in Berlin, Hamburg, and other cities — under the pretext that they could lead to "anti-Semitic hate". Entire student groups have been suspended, posters torn down, events cancelled, and journalists blacklisted.

In October 2023, Berlin police banned a memorial vigil for Palestinian children killed in Gaza, while allowing pro-Israel rallies to proceed uninterrupted. Students from the group Jüdische Stimme, a Jewish anti-Zionist collective, were targeted with hate mail and surveillance, despite their peaceful protest against genocide. Perhaps most disturbingly, Germany has begun deporting or threatening to deport Arab residents and asylum seekers for expressing support for Palestine — a move critics compare to the authoritarian tactics of regimes Germany once condemned.

In this context, the memory of the Holocaust is being weaponised not to prevent genocide, but to silence those who cry out against one.

The Greens and the SPD: A Progressive Façade

Given this repression and complicity, one might reasonably expect such policies from a far-right or conservative government. But they are being carried out by a coalition led by the Social Democratic Party (SPD) and the Greens — parties that claim to uphold progressive values, environmental justice, and human rights.

The SPD's Chancellor Olaf Scholz has defended Israel's "right to self-defence" without conditions, even after entire hospitals were bombed and journalists assassinated. Green Party Foreign Minister Annalena Baerbock has repeated Israeli military justifications verbatim, often without verifying their truth. The Green Party — once known for its pacifist roots — is now justifying arms sales to a state accused of committing genocide.

This betrayal of progressive principles is one of the most shocking aspects of Germany's stance. The very parties who should champion justice for the oppressed have instead folded under ideological pressure and historical guilt, failing to distinguish between the State of Israel and the people of Israel — and equating all criticism of the former with hatred of the latter.

VOICES OF CONSCIENCE: DIE LINKE AND THE GERMAN LEFT

Amid the suffocating conformity of German politics, a few voices still speak out.

Members of Die Linke (The Left Party), along with independent activists, academics, and Jewish anti-Zionists in Germany, have condemned their country's enabling of atrocities. They have protested the banning of demonstrations, called for a halt to arms exports, and challenged the false equivalence between anti-Zionism and antisemitism.

Figures like Heike Hänsel, Diether Dehm, and Sevim Dağdelen have called for Germany to uphold international law and support Palestinian rights, often at great political cost. Jewish Germans like Ronen Steinke and groups such as Jüdische Stimme für gerechten Frieden have risked state and media backlash to remind the public that criticism of Israel is not anti-Semitic — it is an ethical obligation. Germany needs more of this moral clarity — not less.

LEGAL AND ETHICAL ACCOUNTABILITY

Germany's support for Israel during the Gaza war may not only be immoral — it may be illegal. Under international law, supplying weapons with the knowledge that they are being used to commit war crimes constitutes aiding and abetting those crimes.

If the ICJ ultimately rules that Israel is committing genocide in Gaza, countries like Germany that provided military, economic, and diplomatic support could themselves be accused of complicity under the Genocide Convention.

Yet Germany's leaders appear unmoved by this possibility, confident that their political capital and alliance with Washington will shield them from consequences. This arrogance has allowed them to ignore not just the suffering of Gaza but also the voices of their own citizens who demand accountability.

No More in Our Name

Germany has crossed a moral Rubicon. What was once genuine historical repentance has mutated into ideological dogma — one that justifies apartheid, war crimes, and mass murder as long as the perpetrator wears the right flag. This is not what "Never Again" means.

If Germany truly seeks to reckon with its past, it must stand against genocide — no matter who commits it. That means halting all arms exports to Israel, ending the repression of dissent, supporting international investigations, and recentring its foreign policy on human rights rather than historical guilt. Until then, Germany will continue to fund, enable, and legitimise the ongoing suffering of millions. And history, once again, will ask: Where were you when it mattered?

SILENT PARTNERS IN WAR

The UK's Complicity in Gaza's Ordeal

As bombs fall and children are buried beneath rubble in Gaza, the silence of Western democracies has grown deafening. Among the most glaring co-conspirators in this silence is the United Kingdom—not merely a bystander to Israel's brutal campaign in the Occupied Palestinian Territories but a complicit actor. From weapons shipments to diplomatic shielding, economic ties to media narratives, Britain's hands are not clean. This chapter explores the depth and breadth of UK complicity in the ongoing atrocities in Gaza, demanding an urgent reckoning from a nation that claims to champion human rights.

THE COLONIAL ECHO: A HISTORICAL CONTEXT OF BETRAYAL

To understand Britain's modern complicity, one must confront its historical role in the creation of the crisis. The 1917 Balfour Declaration—an imperial promise by Lord Balfour to support a "national home for the Jewish people" in Palestine—was made with no consultation of the land's indigenous Arab population. It paved the way for decades of dispossession, culminating in the 1948 Nakba, when over 700,000 Palestinians were forcibly expelled from their homes during the creation of the Israeli state.

This was no historical footnote. Britain's departure from Mandate Palestine was chaotic and calculated, leaving behind structural fissures and favouring Zionist militias, who were better armed and organised — in part thanks to British tolerance and negligence. In many ways, the UK's colonial legacy is the foundation upon which

Israel's modern apartheid regime was built. But complicity didn't end in 1948. It simply evolved.

ARMING APARTHEID: THE UK'S MILITARY-INDUSTRIAL SUPPORT

Britain is not just a bystander to Israeli military campaigns in Gaza. It is an active supplier of the tools of war. Between 2015 and 2023, the UK licensed at least £446 million worth of military equipment to Israel, including components for fighter jets, drones, targeting systems, ammunition, and armoured vehicles. These are not abstract figures. These are the precise instruments that have been used in repeated bombardments of densely populated areas in Gaza, including hospitals, schools, and refugee camps.

When Israeli F-35 jets strike Gaza's residential blocks, they often do so with British-made components. The UK is part of the F-35 joint strike fighter programme and provides critical parts without which these aircraft cannot function. This makes Britain materially complicit under international law in attacks where these aircraft are used in clear violations of the laws of war.

The UK's own arms export rules prohibit sales where there is a "clear risk" that weapons might be used in serious violations of international humanitarian law. Yet successive Conservative and Labour governments have waved these concerns aside, hiding behind the mantra that Israel has a "right to self-defence" — even when its methods amount to collective punishment.

ECONOMIC ENTANGLEMENTS: PROFITS FROM OCCUPATION

Beyond the arms trade, British corporations continue to profit from the Israeli occupation. Multinational firms headquartered or operating in the UK are embedded in Israel's apartheid economy, particularly in illegal settlements in the West Bank.

Companies such as JCB (a British firm whose bulldozers have been documented by human rights organisations as being used in illegal demolitions of Palestinian homes), Barclays (which has invested in arms manufacturers supplying Israel), and G4S (previously involved in security for Israeli prisons where Palestinian political prisoners are held without charge) reflect a broader pattern of economic support.

The UK government, far from discouraging such entanglements, has actively opposed efforts to challenge them. In 2022, the Conservative government proposed an "anti-boycott bill" that would prevent public bodies—including universities and local councils—from participating in boycotts or divestments targeting Israel. This is not neutrality. It is active repression of peaceful protest against war crimes.

DIPLOMATIC SHIELDING: PROTECTING ISRAEL AT THE INTERNATIONAL STAGE

At the United Nations and other international forums, Britain has consistently shielded Israel from accountability. This includes voting against or abstaining from resolutions condemning Israel's violations of international law, including illegal settlements, disproportionate use of force, and blockade of Gaza.

Following Israel's 2023 and 2024 assaults on Gaza — which saw tens of thousands of civilians killed and critical infrastructure destroyed — the UK repeatedly refused to call for an immediate ceasefire. Instead, UK ministers parroted Israeli talking points about "self-defence" and "human shields", often without any credible evidence.

Even as UN experts described Israel's actions as potentially genocidal, British diplomats remained evasive. When the International Court of Justice began hearing South Africa's genocide case against Israel in 2024, the UK refused to support the proceedings. Instead, it undermined them, issuing vague statements about "respecting international law" while continuing to supply weapons and diplomatic cover.

The UK's silence was not passive; it was strategic – a deliberate effort to insulate Israel from legal and political consequences.

MEDIA NARRATIVES AND THE MANUFACTURE OF CONSENT

Complicity extends beyond the government. Britain's mainstream media—particularly outlets like the BBC, Sky News, and The Times—have played a powerful role in sanitising Israel's actions and framing Palestinians as aggressors, even as their families are incinerated in their own homes.

Headlines emphasise Israeli deaths with visceral detail while reducing Palestinian deaths to statistics. Palestinian voices are marginalised, delegitimised, or demonised, while Israeli military officials are given platforms to justify war crimes with impunity.

This asymmetry shapes public perception and creates a false equivalence between occupier and occupied, aggressor and victim. It also provides the political class with a buffer — an uninformed electorate that sees Gaza's tragedy as distant and inevitable rather than the consequence of deliberate choices made in Westminster and Whitehall.

THE GAZA BLOCKADE AND HUMANITARIAN CRISIS: AIDED AND ABETTED

Gaza has been under a suffocating Israeli-Egyptian blockade since 2007 — a form of collective punishment affecting over 2 million people. This blockade has reduced the territory to what has been described by UN officials as an "open-air prison".

Britain has not only failed to condemn this inhuman policy but has repeatedly supported measures — diplomatically and economically — that reinforce it. It has cut direct aid to UNRWA (the UN agency for Palestinian refugees), delayed support for reconstruction, and parroted Israeli accusations that humanitarian agencies are "complicit with "terror"—without evidence.

In the aftermath of the 2023-2024 siege, Britain's aid response was meagre, delayed, and politically conditional. Rather than call for an end to the blockade, British officials focused on blaming Hamas — ignoring the reality that over half of Gaza's population are children, and the majority of casualties were civilians.

COMPLICITY THROUGH SILENCE: THE OPPOSITION AND CIVIL SOCIETY

Complicity is bipartisan. While the Conservative government has led the charge in arming and defending Israel, the Labour Party under Keir Starmer has done little better. Starmer refused to call for a ceasefire even after the scale of destruction became undeniable and disciplined MPs who supported peaceful protestors or condemned Israeli actions.

This moral cowardice is replicated in British institutions across the board. Universities that teach human rights law simultaneously censor students protesting genocide. Religious institutions issue vague platitudes. Cultural institutions cancel Palestinian artists while hosting Israeli-sponsored festivals.

There are exceptions — tireless activists, journalists, and trade unionists who speak truth to power — but they face a headwind of repression, surveillance, and smear campaigns accusing them of antisemitism for daring to criticise a settler-colonial regime.

A LEGAL RECKONING: IS THE UK VIOLATING INTERNATIONAL LAW?

Given the UK's arms sales, diplomatic cover, and economic support, there is a strong legal argument that it is violating its obligations under international law — particularly the Genocide Convention and the Arms Trade Treaty.

Article III of the Genocide Convention criminalises "complicity in genocide". The ICJ's provisional ruling in the South Africa vs. Israel case has already warned that Israel's actions may plausibly amount to genocide. That raises urgent legal questions for the UK: can it continue supplying arms in the face of such warnings without becoming complicit?

The UK's own domestic courts may soon face these questions, as legal challenges by Palestinian human rights organisations and British lawyers continue to build momentum. Already, public pressure has forced debates in Parliament. But so far, no meaningful shift has occurred.

THE NEED FOR MORAL AND POLITICAL COURAGE

The United Kingdom, once self-styled as a global leader in justice[1], now stands exposed as a silent partner in Gaza's suffering. Through arms, money, silence, and lies, it has enabled one of the most sustained assaults on a civilian population in the 21st century.

Condemnation is not enough. What is required now is a total re-evaluation of UK policy toward Israel-Palestine — grounded not in strategic alliances or colonial guilt, but in international law and human decency.

This means an immediate arms embargo on Israel, diplomatic recognition of Palestinian statehood, support for international investigations, and withdrawal of economic support from companies profiting off occupation and apartheid.

More than that, it means an end to the hypocrisy: Britain cannot claim to support the rules-based international order while financing its collapse in Gaza. To be silent now is to be complicit. And history will remember.

It is especially disheartening that the Labour Party—historically aligned with anti-imperialism and social justice[2] — has become complicit in the suffering of Palestinians. One might reasonably expect a Labour government, or even a Labour opposition, to champion international law, human rights, and resistance to

---

[1] Even a cursory knowledge of colonial history would find such a notion laughable, if it were not such a serious matter.
[2] Though the Irish might quibble with that notion.

militarism. Yet under Keir Starmer's leadership, Labour has echoed Conservative talking points, refused to call for a ceasefire even in the face of catastrophic civilian casualties, and actively suppressed dissent within its own ranks.

This stands in stark contrast to the leadership of Jeremy Corbyn, whose principled stance on Palestinian rights offered a rare and courageous moral clarity in British politics. Corbyn consistently condemned Israeli apartheid, supported peaceful Palestinian resistance, and opposed UK arms sales to Israel — all while facing relentless media vilification and allegations of antisemitism. His commitment to justice, even under immense pressure, represents the kind of political courage sorely lacking in today's opposition benches.

CEASEFIRE EFFORTS AND PEACE PROSPECTS

What's next for Gaza?

The Gaza Strip has been a flashpoint of conflict for decades, enduring repeated cycles of violence, destruction, and humanitarian suffering. Each escalation brings immediate devastation but also renewed international calls for ceasefires and fresh hopes for peace. Yet the path to lasting resolution remains elusive, with complex political, social, and regional dynamics hindering progress.

This chapter explores the current landscape of ceasefire efforts and peace prospects concerning Gaza. It examines past diplomatic initiatives, the roles of key actors, ongoing challenges, and potential pathways forward. In doing so, it seeks to shed light on what might realistically lie ahead for Gaza and its people.

HISTORICAL CONTEXT: THE LONG SHADOW OF CONFLICT

Understanding the prospects for peace in Gaza requires revisiting the roots of the conflict. Since the establishment of Israel in 1948 and the subsequent Palestinian displacement, Gaza has been central to the Israeli-Palestinian struggle.

Following Israel's unilateral disengagement in 2005, when it withdrew settlers and troops, Gaza fell under Hamas control after the 2007 conflict between Hamas and Fatah. Since then, Gaza has been subjected to a blockade by Israel and Egypt, ostensibly for security reasons, but which has contributed to dire economic and humanitarian conditions.

Repeated wars—most notably in 2008–09, 2012, 2014, and more recent escalations—have entrenched animosity and deepened trauma. Ceasefires brokered in each round have provided only temporary calm, as underlying grievances and unresolved political disputes persist.

PAST CEASEFIRES: INTERNATIONAL MEDIATION AND LOCAL AGREEMENTS

Historically, ceasefire agreements have been brokered through various international actors, including Egypt, Qatar, the United Nations, and sometimes the United States.

Egypt has played a particularly significant role, often mediating between Hamas and Israel behind closed doors. Cairo's geographic proximity and political influence allow it to coordinate truce negotiations, facilitate prisoner exchanges, and manage border crossings.

Qatar has also emerged as an important mediator, providing financial support to Gaza and acting as a communication channel between Hamas and the international community.

These ceasefires typically involve immediate halts to hostilities, opening humanitarian corridors, and sometimes limited easing of the blockade. However, they rarely address core political issues such as the status of Gaza, the broader Israeli-Palestinian conflict, or the division between Hamas and the Palestinian Authority.

While ceasefires save lives in the short term, their fragility is evident. They are often reactive—negotiated only after intense violence—rather than proactive peace-building tools.

Key challenges include:

- Mutual distrust: Hamas and Israel view each other with deep suspicion. Hamas resists disarming or recognising Israel, while Israel demands Hamas' demilitarisation as a precondition for negotiations.

- Political fragmentation: The Palestinian political split between Hamas in Gaza and the Palestinian Authority (PA) in the West Bank undermines unified representation in talks.

- Blockade and restrictions: Israel's security concerns lead to continued blockade measures, restricting goods and movement, which fuels resentment and hardship in Gaza.

- External influence: Regional powers such as Iran, Turkey, and Gulf states support different factions, complicating unified peace efforts.

THE OSLO ACCORDS AND BEYOND

The 1993 Oslo Accords were the first major attempt at Israeli-Palestinian peace, establishing the Palestinian Authority and envisioning a two-state solution. However, Gaza remained a contentious area, with Hamas excluded from the process.

Subsequent peace efforts—Camp David 2000, the Roadmap for Peace, and the Annapolis Conference—either excluded Hamas or failed to gain their acceptance, undermining their reach in Gaza.

RECENT INITIATIVES

In recent years, several diplomatic efforts have sought to stabilise Gaza and move toward peace:

- Egyptian-led talks: Egypt has convened rounds of talks focusing on ceasefires, reconstruction, and easing of blockades, especially following major escalations in 2021 and 2023.

- UN-led efforts: The United Nations, through envoys and agencies like UNRWA, pushes for humanitarian access and political dialogue, though its influence on political resolutions remains limited.

- U.S. engagement: Historically a key mediator, the U.S. has often sided closely with Israel but has occasionally attempted to facilitate negotiations or humanitarian aid. However, American domestic politics and shifting priorities affect the consistency of involvement. Besides, America is deeply involved in Israel's wars and cannot be seen as an honest or impartial broker.

- Quartet on the Middle East: Comprising the UN, U.S., EU, and Russia, the Quartet issues statements supporting negotiations but struggles to coordinate unified actions.

PALESTINIAN RECONCILIATION

A critical obstacle to lasting peace is the division between Hamas and the Palestinian Authority. Multiple reconciliation attempts—often mediated by Egypt and Qatar—have faltered over governance, security, and political power.

Without a unified Palestinian leadership that includes Gaza, meaningful negotiations with Israel remain difficult. International actors have often insisted that Hamas must recognise Israel and renounce violence before being included, conditions Hamas has rejected.

REGIONAL AND INTERNATIONAL DIMENSIONS

The Gaza conflict cannot be separated from broader Middle Eastern geopolitics.

ROLE OF NEIGHBOURING COUNTRIES

- Egypt: Balances between security concerns and solidarity with Palestinians; mediates ceasefires and controls the Rafah crossing.

- Israel: Focused on security, deterrence, and maintaining the blockade; wary of Hamas' ties to Iran and Islamist extremism.

- Jordan and Lebanon: Host large Palestinian refugee populations and have stakes in the conflict but limited direct influence on Gaza.

- Iran: Provides financial and military support to Hamas and Palestinian Islamic Jihad, complicating peace efforts.

- Qatar and Turkey: Support Gaza financially and politically, sometimes serving as mediators.

- Gulf States: Shifting diplomatic ties with Israel (e.g., the Abraham Accords) have created new regional dynamics that affect Gaza indirectly.

INTERNATIONAL COMMUNITY

Global powers and organisations provide humanitarian aid, issue diplomatic statements, and occasionally attempt to broker talks. However, geopolitical rivalries, shifting alliances, and competing interests often dilute efforts.

POTENTIAL PATHWAYS TO PEACE: WHAT COULD COME NEXT?

While the challenges are significant, several avenues could shape future peace prospects:

1. Comprehensive ceasefire agreements with monitoring

Creating more durable ceasefires that include clear monitoring mechanisms—possibly through UN peacekeepers or international observers—could reduce the risk of rapid escalation. These agreements would require compromise on border management, prisoner exchanges, and humanitarian access.

2. Palestinian political reconciliation

A unified Palestinian government representing both Gaza and the West Bank is widely regarded as essential. International support for reconciliation, paired with pressure on all parties to moderate positions, could pave the way for joint negotiations.

3. Incremental confidence-building measures

Small, step-by-step measures—such as easing blockade restrictions, allowing more goods and people to move, investing in Gaza's infrastructure, and ceasing punitive measures—can build trust. However, given the widespread destruction of Gaza, this seems extremely unlikely. Nevertheless, economic development projects supported by international donors could reduce poverty and foster stability.

4. Inclusion of Hamas in dialogue

Despite political resistance, some experts argue Hamas must be engaged directly or indirectly in peace talks to achieve lasting agreements.

This may require international guarantees, phased disarmament, or political recognition tied to renunciation of violence.

5. Regional peace frameworks

A broader regional peace process, involving Arab states, could provide guarantees and incentives for all parties. The Abraham Accords and normalisation between Israel and some Gulf states may create new dynamics but also risk marginalising Palestinian concerns if not handled carefully.

While official diplomacy dominates headlines, grassroots peacebuilding efforts in Gaza and Israel also contribute to prospects for peace. Youth organisations, women's groups, and NGOs work across divides to foster dialogue, mutual understanding, and community resilience. Supporting these initiatives alongside high-level talks may create social foundations for peace that endure beyond political agreements.

A FRAGILE BUT NECESSARY HOPE

The future of Gaza hinges on breaking the cycle of violence that has shaped its recent history. Ceasefires provide temporary respite but cannot substitute for political solutions. Lasting peace demands addressing underlying grievances: the blockade, political divisions, security concerns, and the broader Israeli-Palestinian conflict.

While obstacles loom large, multiple actors—including regional neighbours, international mediators, and Gaza's own people—have stakes in achieving peace.

For the tens of thousands of children, families, and communities caught in Gaza's turmoil, peace is not an abstract ideal but a vital necessity. The international community must move beyond reactive ceasefires toward sustained, inclusive dialogue and concrete steps to restore hope and dignity.

Only then can the cycle of war be broken, and Gaza's future be one defined by reconstruction, opportunity, and coexistence rather than conflict and despair.

A Question Once Unthinkable

The Horror in Gaza Has Sparked a Debate on Israel's Right to Exist

For decades, the debate in the West about the Israeli–Palestinian conflict rested on a shared, unquestioned premise: Israel's right to exist as a Jewish state was beyond dispute. Criticism might be levelled at this or that policy — the occupation, the settlements, the blockade of Gaza — but the underlying legitimacy of Israel as a state was treated as inviolable. The only solution imagined was a "two-state solution", where Israel and an independent Palestine would coexist side by side.

Yet today, for the first time since Israel's founding in 1948, a radical question is emerging in the mainstream: does Israel, as it exists and conceives itself, have the right to exist at all? This question — long dismissed as extremist or even anti-Semitic — is being asked not by fringe ideologues alone, but by people in the cultural mainstream: journalists, academics, artists, and young activists, many of them motivated by shock and outrage at the sheer scale of destruction, cruelty, and collective punishment unfolding before their eyes in Gaza.

It is a question freighted with history and pain, and for many, still an unacceptable line to cross. But the fact that it is being asked at all— and not only whispered in radical circles—speaks to the depth of the moral crisis provoked by what the world has seen: children dying of starvation, hospitals bombed, and the deliberate withholding of food, water, and medicine from millions of civilians. In this moment of horror, what was once unthinkable has become, at least, discussable.

The shift did not happen overnight. It is the product of decades of stalled peace talks, expanding settlements, and repeated military assaults on Gaza. But this latest war—marked by the deliberate siege of a civilian population, described by UN officials as "collective punishment"—has shocked even those who had long defended Israel's right to self-defence.

Across social media, horrific images and videos from Gaza circulate daily: malnourished children with distended bellies, entire families killed in an instant by airstrikes, and babies dying because fuel to power incubators was blocked. Western journalists and aid workers have testified to the systematic destruction of homes, schools, and hospitals. Doctors in Gaza speak of amputating children's limbs without anaesthetic because supplies have run out. International law experts, including Jewish scholars and Israeli human rights groups, have warned that these actions amount to war crimes and crimes against humanity.

The effect on public consciousness has been profound. Polls show that especially among younger generations in Europe and North America, sympathy has shifted dramatically toward Palestinians. But the shift goes deeper than sympathy: it has sparked a revaluation of the foundational narrative of Israel itself. How, some now ask, can a state that depends on perpetual violence and dispossession to sustain itself claim a moral right to exist in its present form?

For decades, critics of Israel in the West mostly confined themselves to calls for ending the occupation of the West Bank, lifting the siege on Gaza, or freezing settlement expansion. The two-state solution was seen as the only realistic, just answer. Under this vision, Israel would remain a Jewish state alongside a new Palestinian state.

But the ongoing expansion of settlements, the continued denial of basic rights to Palestinians, and now the devastation of Gaza have led many to doubt whether Israel's political system — which gives Jewish citizens full rights while systematically disenfranchising Palestinians — can ever be reconciled with democratic principles.

The debate has moved, in other words, from "What should Israel do?" to "What is Israel?" And at its heart is a question about the nature of a "Jewish state" in a land where millions of non-Jews live under its control, many of them denied citizenship, movement, or political representation.

THE TENSION IN ISRAEL'S FOUNDING IDEA

To understand this moment, it is important to see the contradiction embedded in Israel's founding: the creation of a specifically Jewish state in a territory already home to an Arab majority. In 1948, when Israel was established, some 750,000 Palestinians were expelled or fled in what they call the Nakba ("catastrophe"). Those who remained became second-class citizens; millions more, their descendants, still live in refugee camps, denied the right to return to their homes.

From the start, Israel's Jewish and democratic character was in tension. To ensure a Jewish majority, it had to limit the return of

146

Palestinian refugees and control population demographics —
measures that, over time, have required increasingly harsh policies:
military occupation, settlement expansion, and siege.

Supporters argued that these measures were necessary for Jewish self-
determination and survival after the Holocaust. But for Palestinians,
the creation of Israel was, and remains, inseparable from their
dispossession.

A GENERATIONAL AND MORAL RECKONING

For older generations in the West, Israel's creation was seen against
the backdrop of European antisemitism and genocide. But younger
people, especially in the age of social media, have come of age seeing
Israel primarily through the lens of occupation, checkpoints,
settlement expansion, and repeated military assaults on Gaza.

For them, the moral frame has shifted: the Holocaust is not forgotten,
but it cannot justify the ongoing oppression of another people.
Increasingly, they see Israel's claim to be both Jewish and democratic
as irreconcilable so long as millions of Palestinians are denied equal
rights.

This is why, for some, the question has moved from "Should Israel
end the occupation?" to "Can a state that privileges one ethno-
religious group over others ever be just?"

BEYOND THE TWO-STATE SOLUTION

The two-state solution, once the consensus goal, now appears to many
as dead. On the ground, Israeli settlements have carved the West Bank
into disconnected enclaves; settlers live under Israeli civil law, while

Palestinians live under military rule. Gaza remains under blockade, and East Jerusalem is increasingly absorbed into Israeli sovereignty.

Even prominent Israeli politicians have declared the two-state solution impossible. Former Prime Minister Naftali Bennett said openly, "I will not give up one centimetre of the Land of Israel." Current far-right ministers call for annexation or expulsion.

In this context, some in the West have begun to ask: if two states are impossible, what then? The alternative would be a single state where Jews and Palestinians have equal rights — an idea that challenges the very notion of Israel as a specifically Jewish state.

IS QUESTIONING ISRAEL'S RIGHT TO EXIST ANTI-SEMITIC?

For many, even raising the question of Israel's right to exist feels dangerous, because it echoes centuries of anti-Semitic denial of Jewish humanity and belonging. Jewish communities worldwide rightly fear that denying Israel's right to exist can slide into denying Jews the right to self-determination.

Yet those now questioning Israel's legitimacy often insist they are not questioning Jewish safety or the existence of a state where Jews live in peace, but the idea of a state that privileges Jews over non-Jews.

They ask: can any ethno-nationalist state, built on the displacement of another people, claim an unconditional right to exist as it is? Or should legitimacy depend on upholding universal human rights?

A DEBATE RESHAPED BY PALESTINIAN VOICES

Part of what makes this moment different is the visibility of Palestinian voices. In the past, the Western debate often took place without Palestinians themselves being heard. Today, Palestinian journalists, academics, and ordinary civilians speak directly to a global audience, documenting their suffering and challenging the idea that their displacement was an unfortunate but necessary price for Jewish self-determination.

They argue: the real question is not whether Israel has a right to exist, but whether Palestinians have a right to exist, to live with dignity and equality in their homeland.

WHY THIS DEBATE MATTERS

For supporters of Israel, this debate can feel like an existential threat. But for many others, it reflects a deeper reckoning with the moral cost of the status quo: millions living under siege, occupation, or as refugees denied return, while another group enjoys full rights.

It is a debate about what kind of world we want to live in: one where the suffering of some can be justified by the security of others, or one that insists on equality and justice for all.

A DANGEROUS MOMENT — AND AN OPPORTUNITY

This is a dangerous moment because it risks deepening divisions and fuelling antisemitism if framed carelessly. But it is also an opportunity to imagine a future beyond endless war and occupation.

Some Palestinian and Israeli thinkers propose a single democratic state with equal rights for all. Others propose a confederation or new models of shared sovereignty. What unites these ideas is a rejection of permanent domination of one group over another.

THE QUESTION WE CANNOT AVOID

The horror in Gaza has forced a question once unthinkable into the open: does any state have an unconditional right to exist if its existence depends on the oppression and displacement of millions? Should a Jewish state built on Palestinian dispossession remain sacrosanct, or should legitimacy be measured by equality and justice?

There are no easy answers. The history is complex, the wounds deep. But in the end, the debate itself may mark a moral awakening: the realisation that true peace cannot be built on the suffering of another people and that no nation — however tragic its past — is exempt from moral scrutiny.

For the first time in decades, the conversation in the West is no longer limited to managing the conflict or restarting "peace talks". It is asking what kind of state can truly be legitimate — and what price, if any, the world is willing to pay to sustain a system built on inequality and dispossession.

History teaches us that the most radical questions, once taboo, sometimes become necessary to ask — not to erase a people, but to imagine a future where everyone, Palestinian and Jew alike, can live with equal rights, dignity, and peace.

PART III
GLOBAL CONSEQUENCES AND GEOPOLITICS

The Gaza Conflict

Impact on Regional Geopolitics

The recurring conflict in Gaza is not an isolated struggle confined within a narrow strip of land; it reverberates across borders, reshaping alliances, challenging regional powers, and influencing international diplomacy. The Gaza conflict's impact on regional geopolitics is complex and multi-layered, touching neighbouring countries, reshaping the calculations of distant powers, and stirring broader debates about identity, security, and power in the Middle East.

This chapter explores how the Gaza conflict affects regional dynamics, examining the perspectives of key neighbouring countries, the wider Arab world, non-Arab regional actors, and major international stakeholders. In doing so, it highlights the intricate interplay of local grievances and global interests that make the Gaza conflict a pivotal force in Middle Eastern geopolitics.

EGYPT: BETWEEN MEDIATOR AND GATEKEEPER

Egypt holds a unique and delicate position in the Gaza conflict. Sharing a border with Gaza at Rafah, it serves as a physical and political gatekeeper for the territory. Cairo has historically played the role of mediator between Israel and Palestinian factions, particularly Hamas.

Egypt's involvement is driven by security concerns, political calculations, and its aspiration to maintain regional influence. The Sinai Peninsula, adjacent to Gaza, has seen years of insurgency fuelled by extremist groups. Egypt fears that unchecked violence in Gaza could spill over, emboldening militant networks.

At the same time, Egypt uses its mediation role to assert its status as a pivotal regional power. Successful brokering of ceasefires or prisoner exchanges often bolsters Cairo's diplomatic standing in the Arab world and in the eyes of Western capitals, especially Washington.

Yet, Egypt's position is not without contradictions. The government under President Abdel Fattah el-Sisi has maintained a complex relationship with Hamas, which emerged from the Muslim Brotherhood — a movement the Egyptian state considers a threat. Thus, Cairo balances between constraining Hamas's military capabilities and preventing a complete collapse of Gaza that could trigger mass displacement into Egyptian territory.

The conflict's escalation often forces Egypt into uncomfortable but necessary diplomatic activism, reaffirming its central but cautious role in Palestinian affairs and the broader Middle Eastern diplomatic chessboard.

JORDAN: A BALANCING ACT SHAPED BY DEMOGRAPHICS

For Jordan, the Gaza conflict resonates deeply within its own population. Nearly half of Jordan's citizens are of Palestinian descent, giving the issue profound domestic significance. Public sentiment in Jordan is overwhelmingly sympathetic to Palestinians, and widespread protests often erupt in response to Israeli military actions in Gaza.

The Jordanian monarchy must navigate this domestic pressure carefully. Amman maintains a peace treaty with Israel, signed in 1994, which is vital for economic and security cooperation. At the same time, the government must demonstrate solidarity with the Palestinian cause to maintain its legitimacy among its people.

The Gaza conflict thus forces Jordan into a tight balancing act: condemning violence against Palestinians while preserving strategic cooperation with Israel, particularly over security matters tied to Jerusalem's holy sites. Any significant escalation in Gaza threatens to inflame tensions within Jordan, challenging the government's stability and its diplomatic posture.

LEBANON: THE SHADOW OF HEZBOLLAH AND BROADER RISKS

Though Lebanon does not share a border with Gaza, the conflict has profound implications for its internal dynamics and regional posture. Lebanon hosts Hezbollah, a powerful Iran-backed militia and political party that frames itself as a defender of Palestinian rights.

During major escalations in Gaza, Hezbollah faces pressure — both internally and from its Iranian allies — to demonstrate solidarity with Palestinian factions. This has sometimes led to limited rocket fire from southern Lebanon into northern Israel, sparking localised clashes.

However, Hezbollah's leadership must weigh these moves carefully. Lebanon is in the midst of a severe economic crisis, and many Lebanese citizens fear being dragged into another large-scale conflict with Israel. The Gaza conflict thus places Hezbollah in a dilemma: balancing its ideological commitment and alliance with Iran against the risk of a broader confrontation that could devastate Lebanon further.

This dynamic underscores how the Gaza conflict can spill beyond direct participants, influencing the calculations of powerful actors like Hezbollah and increasing the risk of multi-front escalation.

ISRAEL: DOMESTIC POLITICS AND STRATEGIC DEPTH

For Israel, the Gaza conflict is both a security challenge and a domestic political issue. Successive Israeli governments have justified military operations as necessary for protecting civilians from rocket attacks launched by Hamas and other factions. Yet, these operations often trigger international criticism and complicate Israel's foreign relations.

Domestically, the Gaza conflict frequently becomes a rallying point in Israeli politics. Leaders across the political spectrum use strong rhetoric on security to appeal to voters, while debates over military strategy and ceasefire negotiations reveal deeper divisions about how to handle Gaza.

Geopolitically, Israel seeks to maintain its normalisation agreements with several Arab states, part of the Abraham Accords signed in 2020. Large-scale violence in Gaza, particularly involving high civilian casualties, risks straining these new relationships, especially when public opinion in countries like the UAE, Bahrain, and Morocco remains deeply supportive of Palestinians.

Thus, the Gaza conflict is central to Israel's security doctrine and regional diplomacy, influencing not only its immediate defence policies but also its broader strategy of integrating into the Arab world.

IRAN: STRENGTHENING THE "AXIS OF RESISTANCE"

For Iran, the Gaza conflict is an opportunity to advance its regional agenda. Tehran positions itself as the primary supporter of the "Axis of Resistance," which includes Hamas, Islamic Jihad, and Hezbollah, among others. By supplying funds, weapons, and training, Iran extends its influence into the Levant and presents itself as the defender of Palestinian rights against Israel.

When violence erupts in Gaza, Iran often steps up its rhetorical support and sometimes accelerates military aid, aiming to enhance its credibility among Arabs and Muslims. This serves Iran's broader goal of challenging U.S. and Israeli influence in the region.

However, Iran's role also carries risks. Its support for groups like Hamas complicates relations with some Arab states, particularly those wary of Iran's ambitions, like Saudi Arabia and Egypt. Still, for Tehran, the Gaza conflict remains a strategic asset: a frontline to project power and distract from its own domestic challenges and international isolation.

TURKEY AND QATAR: COMPETING PATRONAGE AND INFLUENCE

Turkey and Qatar play distinctive roles in Gaza, driven by ideological affinity and geopolitical calculations. Both support Hamas politically and financially, seeing it as part of a broader Islamist movement.

Turkey, under President Recep Tayyip Erdoğan, has used vocal support for Gaza as part of its strategy to claim leadership in the Muslim world. Ankara often denounces Israeli actions and provides humanitarian aid, aiming to bolster its image as a champion of Palestinian rights.

Qatar, meanwhile, has taken on a practical role by funding Gaza's civil services, fuel imports, and reconstruction projects. This allows Doha to position itself as an indispensable mediator while maintaining relationships with both Hamas and Western powers.

The involvement of Turkey and Qatar adds complexity to the conflict, creating multiple patronage networks and sometimes complicating unified Arab responses to crises in Gaza.

THE ARAB WORLD: SHIFTING ALLIANCES AND ENDURING SOLIDARITY

The Gaza conflict continues to resonate powerfully across the Arab world. While some Arab governments, particularly those in the Gulf, have shifted toward pragmatic engagement with Israel, popular solidarity with Palestinians remains strong.

Mass protests often erupt in cities like Amman, Rabat, and Tunis when violence escalates in Gaza, revealing a disconnect between ruling elites and public opinion. This tension forces governments to calibrate their responses carefully: balancing new diplomatic ties with Israel against domestic anger over perceived abandonment of the Palestinian cause.

This dynamic underscores how the Gaza conflict remains a symbol of broader struggles over identity, justice, and sovereignty in the Arab world, making it a persistent geopolitical fault line.

INTERNATIONAL DIMENSIONS: THE UNITED STATES AND BEYOND

The Gaza conflict also affects relations beyond the Middle East. For the United States, Israel's closest ally, the conflict is a recurring diplomatic challenge. Washington typically supports Israel's right to self-defence but faces mounting criticism, particularly from within the Democratic Party and among younger Americans, over Palestinian civilian casualties and the imbalance in U.S. policy.

This shifting domestic debate does not have any significant influence on U.S. foreign policy in spite of growing calls for conditioning aid to Israel or demanding greater protection for civilians.

European countries often find themselves mediating between Israel and the Palestinians diplomatically, while also contending with protests and debates about their own role in the conflict.

Meanwhile, global powers like Russia and China use the Gaza conflict to critique U.S. policy, positioning themselves as alternative brokers or allies to Palestinian factions, though with limited practical influence.

A BROADER GEOPOLITICAL PUZZLE

Ultimately, the Gaza conflict is not merely a local struggle; it is deeply entwined with the region's geopolitical architecture. It shapes the calculations of neighbouring states, empowers or constrains non-state actors, and serves as a symbolic and strategic battlefield in the contest between regional powers.

Egypt and Jordan must balance mediation and domestic stability. Lebanon's Hezbollah navigates solidarity and national interests. Israel contends with security imperatives and diplomatic ambitions. Iran uses the conflict to project power, while Turkey and Qatar see opportunities to expand influence.

Beyond the Middle East, the conflict resonates in the halls of Washington, Brussels, and Moscow, shaping global debates about justice, power, and intervention.

ENDURING IMPACT, UNCERTAIN FUTURE

As long as the underlying causes of the Gaza conflict remain unresolved — from the blockade to the broader Israeli-Palestinian stalemate — its impact on regional geopolitics will persist. The conflict will continue to test old alliances, create new ones, and act as a catalyst for broader regional dynamics. It reminds us that in the Middle East, local struggles rarely stay local for long; they ripple outward, reshaping a region where identity, power, and history remain deeply contested.

In the end, the Gaza conflict is a stark illustration of how even the smallest pieces of land can hold disproportionate geopolitical weight — and why finding a just and lasting solution is not only a moral imperative but a strategic necessity for the entire region and beyond.

FROM GAZA TO GLOBAL ANARCHY

How Impunity for Israel and the U.S. Undermines International Law

In the wake of the devastation unfolding in Gaza, a deeper, quieter disaster is also taking place — one that may prove even more dangerous to humanity in the long run. Beyond the heartbreaking images of bombed hospitals, mass graves, and displaced families, the world is witnessing something more corrosive: the erosion of international law itself.

At the heart of this erosion lies the near-total impunity granted to Israel and, by extension, to the United States — Israel's principal ally and protector. This impunity, built on billions in military aid and a near-automatic veto at the United Nations Security Council, is not simply a regional issue; it signals a global unravelling. If states can commit what leading jurists and human rights experts call war crimes and possibly genocide — and still face no meaningful consequences — what is left of the rules that were meant to restrain the powerful and protect the vulnerable?

The conflict in Gaza is tragic on many levels. But perhaps its most tragic legacy will be this: it exposes how international law, once envisioned as a shield for civilians and a check on state violence, can be rendered toothless by political power. And if the world's most powerful countries can ignore the law when it suits them, why should any state abide by it?

In the ashes of World War II, the world pledged "Never Again." From that vow were born the Geneva Conventions, the Universal Declaration of Human Rights, and the Genocide Convention — legal instruments meant to restrain war, protect civilians, and hold perpetrators of atrocities accountable.

These laws do not demand perfection; war is brutal, and mistakes happen. But they do demand that all sides distinguish between combatants and civilians, avoid disproportionate attacks, and never deliberately target civilians or civilian infrastructure.

For decades, the international community has reaffirmed these rules in treaties, courts, and diplomatic declarations. The International Criminal Court (ICC) was established in 2002 to prosecute genocide, crimes against humanity, and war crimes, even when national courts refuse.

Yet in Gaza, these principles are being openly violated. Civilian neighbourhoods, refugee camps, hospitals and UN shelters have been bombed. Journalists, medics, and aid workers have been killed in unprecedented numbers. More than half of Gaza's population has been displaced, with entire families wiped from civil registries.

And despite detailed evidence from UN agencies, human rights organisations, and journalists on the ground, there is little hope of accountability. Instead, Israeli leaders justify these actions as self-defence, while American officials echo and amplify those justifications, often blocking international calls for ceasefires or investigations.

161

The United States plays a pivotal role in this impunity. It supplies Israel with billions of dollars in military aid, including the very bombs and missiles now flattening Gaza. And when international bodies seek to act — whether by calling for a ceasefire, investigating potential war crimes, or referring matters to the ICC — Washington routinely steps in to block them.

Since the early 1970s, the U.S. has used its veto in the UN Security Council dozens of times to shield Israel from censure or sanctions. In the latest conflict, the Biden administration vetoed or watered down multiple resolutions demanding a halt to military operations, even as civilian casualties soared.

This diplomatic shield, paired with military support, sends a dangerous message: international law applies to others, but not to allies of the United States. It is an inversion of the very principle that all states and all people are equal before the law.

THE DANGER OF DOUBLE STANDARDS

This double standard — where some states face sanctions and prosecution while others act with impunity — corrodes the legitimacy of international law itself.

When Russia invaded Ukraine, Western leaders rightly invoked international law, condemned attacks on civilians, and supported investigations into war crimes. Yet when similar patterns emerge in Gaza — mass displacement, attacks on civilian infrastructure, a siege depriving civilians of food, water, and medicine — the response is different.

To millions across the Global South and in the Arab world, this is not merely hypocrisy; it is proof that international law is not truly universal, but rather an instrument of power wielded by the strong against the weak.

If law becomes a weapon of the powerful rather than a shield for the powerless, it ceases to be law in any meaningful sense. It becomes just another tool in geopolitics.

THE EROSION OF NORMS BEYOND GAZA

The Gaza conflict is a focal point, but the erosion of international law extends far beyond. The same patterns of selective enforcement and impunity appear elsewhere:

- **In Yemen**, U.S. and UK-supplied weapons have been used by Saudi Arabia and the UAE in strikes that killed thousands of civilians.

- **In Afghanistan and Iraq**, American forces and allied contractors committed documented abuses, including torture and unlawful killings, yet few faced prosecution.

- **In Syria**, Russian and Syrian government forces targeted hospitals and civilian infrastructure with little international consequence.

Each instance chips away at the norms that protect civilians. Each signals to authoritarian leaders and armed groups worldwide: if you are powerful, or have powerful friends, you can break the law and escape justice.

The danger is not abstract. If international humanitarian law collapses, the world will become even more dangerous and brutal for civilians.

- **Future wars** may see even fewer restraints, as states realise that targeting civilians, blockading food and medicine, or destroying entire cities will not bring legal or political consequences.

- **Armed groups** may justify atrocities by pointing to the conduct of states that were never punished.

- **Global institutions** from the UN to the ICC risk irrelevance if they are seen as powerless or biased.

And in the long run, the security of even powerful states will suffer. A world without rules is a world where violence spreads, where displaced populations grow, and where the next conflict becomes harder to contain.

VOICES WARNING OF COLLAPSE

Legal scholars, UN experts, and even some Western officials have raised an alarm. UN Secretary-General António Guterres has warned of "a crisis of credibility" for international law. Prominent human rights lawyers argue that the Gaza conflict risks normalising collective punishment and attacks on civilians.

The International Court of Justice, in its provisional measures in South Africa's genocide case against Israel, acknowledged a "plausible risk of genocide" and ordered Israel to prevent such acts. Yet enforcement depends on political will — and Washington's continued support has rendered the ruling largely symbolic.

These warnings should not be ignored. The erosion of norms is not a distant threat; it is happening now, and its effects will endure.

RESTORING THE LAW: WHAT MUST BE DONE

Preventing a slide into lawlessness requires more than condemnation; it requires concrete action:

1. End impunity for all:

Accountability must apply equally, whether crimes are committed by allies or adversaries. This means supporting, not undermining, investigations into alleged war crimes and potential genocide — including by the ICC.

2. Condition military aid:

States providing weapons must ensure they are not used to commit violations of international law. This means ending or conditioning arms transfers when there is a clear risk of misuse.

3. Strengthen international institutions:

The UN Security Council's veto power, often abused by permanent members, undermines accountability. Reforming this system — or creating alternative mechanisms for investigation and prosecution — is essential.

4. Reassert norms in public discourse:

Leaders, media, and civil society must resist dehumanising narratives that justify violence against civilians, whether in Gaza, Ukraine, or elsewhere.

5. Invest in justice mechanisms:

Universal jurisdiction, better funding for international courts, and national prosecutions can help close accountability gaps.

A MORAL AND STRATEGIC IMPERATIVE

Some argue that supporting Israel's actions in Gaza is a strategic necessity or a matter of loyalty to an ally. But undermining international law ultimately harms everyone — including Israel and the United States.

For Israel, impunity deepens cycles of violence and alienates global opinion. For the U.S., it damages moral authority, fuels anti-American sentiment, and undermines the very legal norms that protect American soldiers and citizens abroad. A world without rules is not safer for the powerful; it is more dangerous for all.

THE CHOICE BEFORE US

The Gaza conflict lays bare a stark choice: uphold the universal principles that emerged from humanity's darkest hours, or abandon them to the dictates of power.

Impunity for Israel and the U.S. does not merely betray Palestinian civilians; it betrays the entire post-World War II promise of a world governed by law, not might. And the price of that betrayal will not be paid only in Gaza. It will be paid wherever the next leader, general, or militia decides that international law is just words on paper. If we allow this to stand, the world we leave to the next generation will be more violent, more unjust, and ultimately more insecure. The stakes could not be higher. The time to act — to restore the force of law and the universality of justice — is now.

GENOCIDE IN THE DIGITAL AGE

Global Silence and Selective Outrage

A mother in Gaza films herself hugging her children in the final moments before an airstrike flattens their home, a teenager livestreams from a collapsing hospital, pleading for help that never comes. As the world scrolls past these moments on TikTok, Instagram, and X, a question hangs heavy: why does the world watch genocide unfold — and do nothing?

In an era when information is instant, the unfolding devastation in Gaza exposes a darker truth: technology does not guarantee justice, and outrage does not always lead to action. The world's selective empathy, shaped by politics, prejudice, and digital algorithms, reveals why some lives are mourned while others are silently erased.

AN ATROCITY VISIBLE IN REAL TIME

Unlike past genocides — in Rwanda, Bosnia, or Cambodia — the horror in Gaza has been documented moment by moment by those living through it. Videos emerge within minutes: a father wailing over the body of his child, doctors operating under a flashlight, entire neighbourhoods turned to dust.

These images spread faster than official statements, news reports, or diplomatic condemnations. Palestinians have become both victims and chroniclers, using smartphones as the only weapons they possess against erasure. As bombs fall, they upload proof to the world.

Yet despite this flood of evidence, international institutions, major powers, and even some global media remain hesitant to name what they see: a genocide unfolding in real time.

WHAT MAKES IT GENOCIDE?

The term "genocide" was coined by Raphael Lemkin in 1944, defined legally as acts committed with the intent to destroy, in whole or in part, a national, ethnic, racial, or religious group. In Gaza, human rights experts and international legal scholars argue that Israel's sustained bombardment, mass displacement, and deliberate targeting of essential life systems meet this threshold.

Statements by Israeli officials calling Palestinians "human animals," vowing to make Gaza "disappear," or describing a goal of "total destruction" have been cited as evidence of genocidal intent. UN experts, South Africa's case before the International Court of Justice (ICJ), and dozens of human rights organisations have echoed this concern. Yet many Western governments refuse to use the term, sticking to language like "self-defence" or "regrettable civilian casualties."

SELECTIVE OUTRAGE AND THE HIERARCHY OF VICTIMS

Part of Gaza's tragedy lies not just in the violence, but in how the world reacts. When Russia invaded Ukraine, Western nations swiftly imposed sanctions, sent weapons, and welcomed refugees with open arms. Leaders spoke passionately about defending human rights and international law.

In contrast, Palestinian suffering often meets silence, excuses, or condemnation of "both sides." Palestinian refugees find few doors open. Military aid to Israel continues, even as bombs flatten schools and hospitals.

This disparity reveals a deeper hierarchy of victims, shaped by geopolitics, racism, and media framing. Palestinian voices are routinely doubted, their deaths depersonalised into numbers, while Israeli casualties are named, photographed, and mourned globally.

THE DIGITAL BATTLEFIELD

Social media offered hope that marginalised voices could finally reach the world. And indeed, Gazans have made the suffering impossible to deny. Hashtags trend; millions share heartbreaking videos; global protests erupt. But the same platforms also suppress Palestinian content. Reports show widespread takedowns, shadow-bans, and algorithmic throttling of posts about Gaza, often justified by vague "community guidelines." Meanwhile, misinformation and state-backed propaganda spread unchecked. The result is a paradox: a genocide that is both the most documented in history and the most digitally censored.

THE COMFORT OF NEUTRALITY

Many institutions — media outlets, universities, and even humanitarian organisations — retreat into "neutrality." They warn staff against using words like "genocide," "apartheid," or "occupation." Statements are carefully balanced: "We condemn violence on both sides."

But neutrality, as Desmond Tutu famously warned during South Africa's apartheid, almost always supports the status quo. In Gaza, it means ignoring the power imbalance between an occupying military

170

and a besieged civilian population. Neutral language shields not only Israel from accountability but also the world's conscience from guilt.

THE PRICE OF SPEAKING OUT

Those who name Gaza's destruction as genocide often face severe backlash: journalists fired, professors disciplined, activists doxxed or threatened. To say that activists are being doxxed means that someone is publicly revealing their private or personal information on the internet (such as home addresses, phone numbers, email addresses, or even family details) without their consent — usually with the intention to harass, intimidate, or threaten them. Western politicians risk being labelled anti-Semitic or accused of "supporting terrorism." This climate of fear deepens silence. Even Jewish groups critical of Israel's war face ostracism, revealing that the real red line is not hate speech but questioning state violence, especially Zionism.

VOICES FROM GAZA

Beyond the headlines, Palestinians in Gaza continue to document their lives under siege. A young poet posts verses about hope among the ruins, a doctor livestreams surgeries on bomb-shattered children, a father, digging through rubble, begs the world to remember his family's names. They do not speak in diplomatic language. Their words are raw, personal, and accusatory: *"You see us dying. Why won't you stop it?"* Their testimony, archived forever online, challenges historians and future generations: you cannot say you didn't know.

THE COMPLICITY OF THE POWERFUL

Genocide does not happen in isolation. It requires complicity: weapons shipments, diplomatic cover, and media narratives that dehumanise the victims. The U.S.A., UK, and EU states continue to supply arms and block ceasefire resolutions. Arab governments, once loud in rhetoric, now largely remain silent or focus on their own regional alliances.

Meanwhile, international bodies like the UN issue warnings and reports, but lack enforcement power. The ICJ's emergency orders to prevent genocide in Gaza remain largely ignored.

WHAT WOULD ACCOUNTABILITY LOOK LIKE?

Ending genocide requires more than outrage. It demands tangible actions: arms embargoes, sanctions, prosecutions of those who incite or carry out mass atrocities, and ultimately, dismantling the structures of occupation and blockade. It also means listening to Palestinians, not as symbols of tragedy but as people with agency, history, and rights.

HOPE, EVEN NOW

Despite the horror, there are signs of change. Millions worldwide, from Johannesburg to Jakarta, march for Gaza. Jewish and Palestinian activists stand side by side demanding a ceasefire. Survivors of other genocides speak out in solidarity.

The digital age makes erasure harder. Archives, testimonies, and videos create a permanent record that future generations cannot ignore.

Yet the question remains whether this visibility can overcome political interests and systemic racism — whether watching can become action.

A WORLD REFLECTED IN GAZA

The catastrophe in Gaza is more than a local tragedy. It reflects global failures: of international law corrupted by power, of media captured by state narratives, and of societies that value some lives over others.

As bombs keep falling and videos keep streaming, the world faces a choice: remain passive spectators or confront the systems that allow genocide to happen before our eyes. For the people filming under fire, the question is not whether history will remember — but whether history will judge those who watched and stayed silent.

"One day," wrote Palestinian journalist Yasser Murtaja before being killed by an Israeli sniper, "I will take this camera and show the world how beautiful Gaza can be."

In the digital age, the evidence of genocide is undeniable. The real test is whether the world, so quick to tweet, will finally act.

THE ROLE OF MEDIA NARRATIVES

Shaping Public Opinion on Gaza

In an age when a single photograph can go viral within minutes, the conflict in Gaza is not just fought with rockets and ceasefires but also through headlines, hashtags, and nightly news segments. Media narratives play a central role in shaping how millions around the world understand — and often misunderstand — the reality on the ground.

These narratives are not monolithic. They vary sharply across regions, languages, editorial policies, and ideological leanings. The ways in which media outlets frame the conflict in Gaza deeply influence public opinion, policy debates, and even diplomatic strategies. This chapter explores how different media narratives emerge, why they diverge, and the consequences of these portrayals on global understanding and action.

THE POWER OF FRAMING: WHY NARRATIVES MATTER

Every conflict is also a battle over narrative: who is perceived as the aggressor, who as the victim, and which historical and political context is foregrounded or ignored. In the case of Gaza, these narratives are particularly polarised.

Framing is the process by which media shape a story by choosing what to highlight, what to omit, and which words and images to use. For instance, describing an airstrike as a "response" implies defence, while calling it an "attack" implies aggression. Referring to civilian deaths as "casualties" can appear neutral, while "killing of civilians" sounds more condemnatory. Such linguistic and editorial choices, repeated across millions of screens and pages, create deeply ingrained perceptions that influence public sentiment and political discourse.

WESTERN MEDIA: BALANCING ACT OR IMBALANCE?

In many Western countries, major media outlets often frame the conflict through a lens of symmetry: presenting it as "clashes between Israel and Hamas" or "escalations between Israelis and Palestinians." This framing suggests an equivalence of power and responsibility that critics argue does not reflect the realities on the ground.

Coverage in outlets like the BBC, CNN, or The New York Times frequently leads with headlines about rocket attacks on Israeli cities, often emphasising the threat to Israeli civilians before mentioning Palestinian casualties. While reports do cover destruction and suffering in Gaza, the sequencing can subtly shape viewers' perception of who is under greater threat.

Several factors contribute to this framing:

- Editorial caution: In politically charged conflicts, media organisations fear accusations of bias and strive for "balance" by presenting both sides equally, even if the situation is asymmetric.

- Reliance on official sources: Western journalists often draw statements from the Israeli government, military spokespeople, and U.S. State Department officials, whose narratives frame actions as defensive.

- Accessibility: Israel generally allows foreign journalists more freedom of movement and access, whereas entering Gaza is logistically and politically harder, particularly during escalations.

Over time, these factors create a structural bias — not necessarily driven by malice, but by institutional and practical constraints — that privileges certain narratives over others.

In contrast, media outlets based in Palestine and across the Arab world often focus on the human impact in Gaza. Channels like Al Jazeera Arabic, Al Mayadeen, and Palestine TV prioritise images and testimonies of destroyed homes, injured civilians, and funerals. This coverage centres the disproportionate suffering in Gaza and places it within a broader narrative of occupation and historical injustice. The emphasis is often on the lack of basic human rights, the blockade's humanitarian toll, and the continuity of displacement since 1948.

Language is also instructive. Where Western outlets might say "airstrikes hit targets in Gaza," Arab media more frequently use "bombardment of civilian areas." The word choice reflects a worldview in which the conflict is fundamentally about power imbalance and enduring occupation. This narrative resonates deeply with audiences across the Arab and Muslim worlds, shaping solidarity movements, protests, and diplomatic positions.

ISRAELI MEDIA: NATIONAL SECURITY AND INTERNAL DEBATE

Within Israel, media coverage focuses heavily on national security and the immediate impact of rocket attacks on Israeli civilians. Reports highlight damage to homes, psychological trauma, and the heroism of first responders.

Israeli media are diverse, but in spite of that, internal debates about government policy, military tactics, and ethics are not as robust or impartial as one might expect. Nevertheless, outlets like Haaretz provide some level of critical reporting on the impact of military operations in Gaza and offer limited space for Palestinian voices, while more right-leaning publications like Israel Hayom adopt a government-aligned perspective, emphasising deterrence and defence.

It is a matter of shock and horror that surveys reveal that the majority of Israelis support the war on Gaza and wish to see the complete destruction of Gaza. But considering how Israeli media manipulates and frames reportage, it might be that they are being steered in a particular direction that influences their perceptions and responses.

Recent surveys among Israelis show that a large majority of Jewish Israelis continue to back the war on Gaza, largely viewing it as a justified response to Hamas's attacks. For example, polling from the Israel Democracy Institute in late 2023 found nearly 90% support for the military campaign. At the same time, other surveys have revealed troubling attitudes: around 82% of Jewish Israelis favoured forcibly expelling Gaza's residents, and about 47% agreed with a statement advocating killing all inhabitants of a conquered enemy city—though this was framed as a hypothetical scenario rather than an explicit policy proposal. Despite strong support for the war itself, more recent polling indicates that many Israelis would prefer ending the conflict through a deal to secure the return of hostages rather than pursuing absolute military victory.

For Israeli audiences, the prevailing narrative often frames military actions as regrettable but necessary, driven by Hamas's rocket fire and stated aim to "destroy Israel." Civilian casualties in Gaza are typically portrayed as tragic but inevitable consequences of Hamas's alleged use of civilian areas to launch attacks.

Social media has transformed the information landscape, challenging traditional media narratives and amplifying voices previously excluded from mainstream coverage. During escalations, residents of Gaza post real-time updates, videos of destroyed neighbourhoods, and personal testimonies that quickly circulate globally. Hashtags like #GazaUnderAttack and #FreePalestine trend worldwide, drawing attention to civilian suffering. Conversely, Israeli social media users share videos of rockets hitting cities like Ashkelon and Tel Aviv, images of people sheltering, and stories of those killed or injured.

Activists and influencers play a crucial role, reaching audiences who may not follow traditional news outlets. Celebrities sharing posts about Gaza can spark debates and raise awareness, though sometimes at the cost of oversimplifying complex realities.

Yet social media is also a battleground for disinformation. Fabricated images, misleading videos, and out-of-context footage spread quickly, sometimes shaping perceptions more powerfully than verified journalism. Both sides, as well as external actors, have been accused of manipulating social media narratives to serve political aims. This would be a less significant issue if international journalists were allowed into Gaza.

HISTORICAL NARRATIVES: MEMORY AND CONTEXT

Media narratives about Gaza do not emerge in a vacuum; they are deeply rooted in historical memory and national narratives. For many Palestinians and Arabs, Gaza is not merely a territory but a symbol of resistance against occupation and dispossession. Coverage reflects a historical continuum, linking current suffering to the Nakba of 1948, when hundreds of thousands of Palestinians were displaced.

In Israeli media and political discourse, Gaza is often framed as a security threat emerging after Israel's 2005 disengagement, when settlements were evacuated and Hamas rose to power. This narrative sees rocket attacks as confirmation that territorial concessions bring insecurity.

Western media narratives often mirror the lack of deep historical context common in Western public consciousness. Coverage tends to focus on recent escalations, sometimes without reference to decades of occupation, displacement, or blockade. This omission can shape public understanding in subtle but significant ways, turning systemic issues into episodic "flare-ups."

HUMANISING VS. DEHUMANISING: THE IMPACT OF VISUALS AND LANGUAGE

One of the most powerful aspects of media coverage is its ability to humanise — or dehumanise — people in conflict zones. Photos of grieving families, wounded children, or destroyed homes create empathy and outrage. Conversely, abstract language — "targets hit," "collateral damage" — can distance audiences from human suffering.

Studies have shown that naming victims, sharing their stories, and showing their faces increases public engagement and empathy. In contrast, focusing primarily on military statistics or anonymous casualties reduces emotional impact.

Who gets humanised matters: stories about Israeli victims are often detailed in Western media, including names, ages, and family backgrounds, while Palestinian casualties are sometimes presented as numbers. This imbalance can shape who audiences see as fully human and whose suffering is understood as regrettable but impersonal.

INFLUENCE ON POLICY AND PUBLIC OPINION

Media narratives directly affect how citizens view the conflict and what they demand from policymakers. In the United States, shifts in media coverage — including greater inclusion of Palestinian voices and criticism of Israeli policies — have contributed to changing public opinion, particularly among younger Americans and progressives. This has led to more vocal debates in Congress and calls to condition military aid.

In Europe, media coverage highlighting humanitarian crises in Gaza fuels public protests and pushes governments to call for ceasefires or condemn disproportionate use of force.

In the Arab world, emotionally charged coverage sustains popular solidarity with Palestinians and constrains leaders from pursuing closer ties with Israel without addressing Palestinian rights.

THE ETHICAL CHALLENGE: REPORTING ON ASYMMETRIC CONFLICT

Journalists face complex ethical dilemmas when covering Gaza. How to remain objective while reporting on overwhelming human suffering? How to verify information in a territory with limited access? How to challenge official narratives without endangering local contacts or staff?

Moreover, media organisations must decide whether striving for "balance" in coverage of an asymmetric conflict can unintentionally obscure the reality of power disparities.

Some media critics argue that "objectivity" should not mean presenting an occupier and an occupied as equally responsible, but rather reflecting the facts and context accurately, even if they challenge powerful interests.

TOWARD MORE NUANCED COVERAGE

There are signs of evolution. In recent years, some Western outlets have included more Palestinian perspectives and critical analysis of policies like the blockade. Terms once considered controversial, like "occupation" or "apartheid," now appear more frequently in mainstream discourse, reflecting the influence of human rights organisations and academic research. Yet challenges remain: editorial pressures, fear of political backlash, and the rapid pace of digital news can still lead to incomplete or distorted narratives.

NARRATIVES AS POWER

The conflict in Gaza illustrates a broader truth: media narratives do not just reflect reality; they help construct it. They shape how the world sees a conflict, whose suffering is visible, and whose voices are heard.

For audiences, the challenge is to seek out diverse sources, question framing, and look beyond headlines to understand the human and historical complexity of Gaza.

For journalists and media organisations, the task is to navigate political pressures, logistical barriers, and ethical dilemmas to tell stories that do justice to those living under siege and fear.

In the end, narratives are not mere words and images. They shape empathy, anger, apathy, and ultimately, the political will to demand change — or to look away.

WHO CONTROLS THE STORY?

Western Media and the Framing of Gaza

In war, truth is the first casualty — but who decides what counts as truth? Every day, Gaza's devastation unfolds in front of billions: a mother cradling her dead child, a bombed hospital turned into a morgue, an elderly man searching for family beneath rubble. Yet in many Western media outlets, the words used to describe this horror often carry a strange distance: "Israeli strikes hit targets in Gaza." "Hamas-run health ministry says." "Clashes erupt."

Language shapes perception. And in the story of Gaza, language often shifts responsibility, obscures power, and reframes aggression as tragic inevitability. Behind every headline lies a deeper question: who controls the story of Gaza, and why does it matter?

THE POWER OF FRAMING

Words like "conflict," "clashes," and "both sides" suggest symmetry, implying two equal forces locked in a tragic struggle. But Gaza is not symmetrical. It is a besieged enclave whose population — mostly refugees from the 1948 Nakba — lives under military blockade and occupation. Israel, by contrast, is a nuclear-armed state with one of the world's most advanced militaries.

Yet coverage often strips away this context. An airstrike that destroys an entire family home becomes "an exchange of fire." The deaths of Israeli civilians are humanised with names, photos, and personal stories. Palestinian casualties are numbers, reported by "the Hamas-run health ministry" — a subtle disclaimer that invites doubt.

183

This framing matters. It shapes public understanding, political debate, and ultimately, policy decisions that can mean life or death.

OCCUPATION BECOMES INVISIBLE

One of the most striking omissions in mainstream reporting is the word "occupation." While international law and UN resolutions clearly describe Gaza and the West Bank as occupied territories, many outlets use softer terms like "disputed" or avoid the subject altogether.

This erasure transforms Palestinian resistance into unprovoked aggression, rather than a response to decades of military rule, land confiscation, and displacement. Without context, rockets fired from Gaza appear senseless; with context, they appear as desperate acts in an asymmetric struggle.

As Palestinian-American writer Yousef Munayyer notes: "Without explaining why Palestinians resist, coverage makes it seem like violence erupts out of cultural rage, not political oppression."

THE PROBLEM OF SOURCES

News reports rely heavily on official sources: government statements, military briefings, and Western diplomatic comments. Israeli officials are quoted as authoritative voices; Palestinian officials, especially from Hamas, are often framed as biased or unreliable.

When Gaza's health ministry reports casualties, many headlines include disclaimers like "according to Hamas." Yet Israeli military statements — even when later proven false — often run unchallenged.

This imbalance reflects a broader media culture that privileges certain voices over others, shaped by geopolitical alliances, institutional biases, and access. Journalists covering Gaza often cannot enter due to Israeli and Egyptian restrictions; those reporting from Tel Aviv enjoy carefully choreographed press conferences and direct statements from government spokespeople.

VISUAL BIASES

Images tell stories that words cannot. But even visual coverage often reinforces asymmetry. Photos of Israeli casualties tend to show individuals: grieving families, funerals, destroyed homes. Images from Gaza more often depict crowds, rubble, and masked fighters — scenes that feel distant, collective, and depersonalised.

These choices are rarely conscious conspiracies, but rather reflect editorial instincts shaped by decades of framing the conflict through an Israeli-centric lens.

HISTORICAL ERASURE

Coverage of Gaza rarely traces the roots of its crisis: the Nakba, the occupation of 1967, or the blockade imposed since 2007. Instead, violence is presented as a cycle of revenge between ancient enemies.

By ignoring the historical context, the media transforms political demands — freedom, self-determination, and an end to occupation — into religious fanaticism or hatred. The Palestinian narrative becomes trapped in a frame of terror rather than rights. As Edward Said warned, "The question is not whether Palestinians exist, but whether they are allowed to represent themselves."

THE TERRORISM FRAME

When Palestinians use violence, it is almost universally labelled "terrorism." Israeli violence, even when massively disproportionate, is described as "retaliation" or "self-defence." This framing both dehumanises Palestinians and absolves Israel of responsibility. Civilian deaths in Gaza are called "collateral damage." Palestinian fighters are "militants" or "terrorists," even when resisting military occupation — a right recognised under international law. The word "terrorist" itself, famously flexible, is rarely applied to state actors, though states often commit the deadliest acts.

WHY IT PERSISTS

This bias is not only about individual journalists. It is systemic, shaped by several forces:

- **Political pressure:** Media outlets fear accusations of antisemitism if they criticise Israel too directly.

- **Economic interests:** Owners and advertisers may align with political elites supportive of Israel.

- **Institutional habits:** Reporters often start in Jerusalem or Tel Aviv, building relationships with Israeli officials.

- **Access:** Israel controls entry to Gaza; angering Israeli authorities risks losing credentials.

Together, these pressures reinforce a cautious, state-centric approach.

SILENCING PALESTINIAN VOICES

Palestinian journalists and activists face disproportionate risks. Since October 2023, dozens of Palestinian journalists have been killed. Many Western outlets still rely on Israeli or foreign correspondents rather than local voices, perpetuating an imbalance. Even when Palestinian perspectives are included, they are often framed as "emotional reactions," while Israeli analysts provide the "objective" political analysis. The result is not total censorship, but a structural filter that narrows acceptable narratives.

CHALLENGING THE FRAME

Some journalists and outlets break these patterns. Independent media, human rights organisations, and Palestinian reporters offer alternative coverage centred on power, law, and human impact. Social media has allowed Palestinians to speak directly to global audiences. A mother's livestream from Gaza, a child's plea on TikTok — these personal stories can bypass institutional filters.

Yet platforms also censor Palestinian content, often under vague "violence" or "terrorism" policies. Reports document thousands of removed posts, throttled hashtags, and suspended accounts.

A BROADER MEDIA CRISIS

The coverage of Gaza is part of a wider crisis: a media system that struggles to hold power accountable, especially when power is Western or allied. It is easier to denounce the Russian bombing of Ukrainian cities than the Israeli bombing of Gaza, though both kill civilians in their homes. The difference reflects not objective standards, but political alignments. The cost is borne by ordinary people whose suffering is either spotlighted or shadowed, depending on who bombs them.

WHAT WOULD BALANCED COVERAGE LOOK LIKE?

True balance is not counting quotes from "both sides." It is centring those most affected, providing historical context, naming occupation and apartheid, and questioning power. It means calling things what they are: describing ethnic cleansing, war crimes, and state violence without euphemisms. It also means recognising Palestinian humanity beyond victimhood — their culture, humour, resilience, and demands for justice.

THE STAKES OF THE STORY

Stories shape reality. How media frames Gaza influences whether governments feel pressured to act, whether citizens protest, and whether future atrocities can be justified. When occupation becomes invisible, resistance seems irrational. When genocide becomes "clashes," stopping it seems less urgent. As journalist Mohammed El-Kurd writes, "The media doesn't just report on Gaza; it builds the walls that keep Gaza besieged."

BEYOND HEADLINES

Media bias alone cannot explain Gaza's catastrophe, but it is a powerful pillar upholding the status quo. Dismantling it requires not only better reporting but challenging deeper structures: colonial legacies, military alliances, and racial hierarchies. Ultimately, the question is not just who tells Gaza's story — but whether we listen, and what we do with what we hear. "We Palestinians do not want to be symbols," writes writer Refaat Alareer, killed in Gaza in 2023. "We want to be people, living our ordinary lives."

In telling Gaza's story, the media can choose to trap Palestinians in an endless frame of violence — or finally show the reality of occupation, humanity, and hope.

WHEN CONSCIENCE SPEAKS

The Tide of Public Opinion is Turning Against Israel

In recent months, the tide of public opinion toward Israel has shifted in a way that would have seemed unimaginable only a few years ago. What once was an unquestioned stance among much of the Western public—reflexive support for Israel—has fractured under the weight of grim realities coming out of Gaza. Images and testimonies of horror have circulated around the world: children dying under rubble, the wounded undergoing amputations without anaesthesia, families starving as entire neighbourhoods are reduced to dust. Hospitals have been bombed or besieged, humanitarian workers killed, and water, food, and medicine deliberately withheld from an entire population.

Among those leading this profound shift are artists, writers, musicians, and actors—people whose voices carry cultural weight and who have historically shaped public sentiment. Their statements, open letters, and actions have helped crystallise a broader realisation: what is unfolding is not an unfortunate by-product of war, but collective punishment and a humanitarian catastrophe that cannot be morally defended.

This shift is neither sudden nor isolated. It is the culmination of years of frustration and horror over policies that treat Palestinian life as expendable, now starkly highlighted by an offensive whose human cost is documented daily by journalists, doctors, and residents risking (and often losing) their lives to bear witness.

While criticism of Israeli policy has existed for decades, what has distinguished this moment is its breadth and urgency. Reports from Gaza detail entire families being wiped out in a single airstrike. According to humanitarian agencies, over half the population faces starvation conditions; children's bodies show signs of extreme malnutrition, and infectious diseases spread among the displaced living in makeshift tents.

Doctors Without Borders (MSF) and the World Health Organisation have reported surgeries on children performed without anaesthesia due to the blockade of medical supplies. UN officials have described the crisis as "a living hell." In May, the UN Special Rapporteur on the Occupied Palestinian Territories accused Israel of committing war crimes and crimes against humanity, citing deliberate targeting of civilians and destruction of infrastructure essential for life.

Images from Gaza show mothers writing their children's names on their limbs so they can be identified after death. Videos of dust-covered, screaming children rescued from ruins have flooded social media, bypassing traditional media filters and searing into the conscience of millions.

THE COLLECTIVE PUNISHMENT OF A PEOPLE

Central to this outrage is the sense that what is happening in Gaza is not simply a tragic consequence of conflict but a policy of collective punishment. The Israeli government has openly acknowledged it would impose a "complete siege" on Gaza, cutting off food, water, fuel, and electricity to force Hamas to release hostages. Yet the punishment falls overwhelmingly on civilians who have no control over political or military decisions.

This is not a theoretical debate. It is about real people: premature babies dying in incubators as electricity fails; cancer patients left to die untreated; mothers giving birth in unsanitary tents; children psychologically scarred by constant bombardment.

Such realities have forced even those who once saw Israel as a necessary bulwark against terrorism to ask: at what moral cost? Can any cause justify the starvation of millions, the killing of thousands of children, and the destruction of an entire society's future?

ARTISTS AND CULTURAL FIGURES SPEAK OUT.

Against this backdrop, cultural figures have found their voices—and their influence is significant. From actors and musicians to writers and filmmakers, a chorus of condemnation has risen, often at great personal and professional risk.

In Hollywood, actors like Susan Sarandon, Mark Ruffalo, and Bella Hadid have denounced the bombing of Gaza and called for a ceasefire. Screenwriters, directors, and producers have signed open letters demanding an end to the killing. Musicians including Dua Lipa, Macklemore, and Killer Mike have used their platforms to highlight Palestinian suffering.

In the literary world, hundreds of writers—including Pulitzer Prize winners and bestselling novelists—have signed letters accusing Israel of crimes against humanity and condemning Western governments for their complicity. The art world has seen similar activism: prominent curators and artists have pulled out of cultural events or refused to collaborate with institutions seen as supporting Israeli policy.

Perhaps most striking is the tone of these statements: not measured diplomatic language, but words of moral urgency and outrage. The repeated theme is simple: silence in the face of such atrocities is complicity.

CENSORSHIP AND BACKLASH—AND WHY IT HASN'T WORKED

These cultural figures have not spoken out without consequence. Many have faced fierce backlash: loss of contracts, smear campaigns in the media, even threats to their safety. Organisations have attempted to silence criticism by branding it as anti-Semitic—a deeply damaging tactic that conflates opposition to Israeli government policy with hatred of Jewish people.

Yet the scale and intensity of the crisis in Gaza have made these attempts at suppression less effective. Artists who might have stayed silent before now feel compelled to speak out, not because it is safe, but because their conscience demands it. The sight of children dying from dehydration and starvation is a moral alarm bell too loud to ignore.

SOCIAL MEDIA AND THE EROSION OF THE OLD NARRATIVE

One reason for this shift is the democratisation of information. Social media has made it impossible to fully control the narrative. Palestinian journalists and civilians in Gaza have documented their own suffering in real time, creating an unfiltered record that challenges official statements.

When mainstream media outlets fail to report or underreport, the gap is filled by citizen journalism. This has led to a growing scepticism of official narratives and a greater willingness to listen to Palestinian voices that were once marginalised.

A GENERATIONAL DIVIDE

Polls show a striking generational divide in attitudes toward Israel. Among younger people in the U.S., support for Israel has fallen dramatically, while sympathy for Palestinians has grown. The same trend is seen in Europe and many other parts of the world.

This younger generation, raised on global social media, is less influenced by old geopolitical frameworks and more driven by clear moral intuitions: when they see children starving, they ask who is responsible. The answer, documented by human rights organisations, is increasingly clear.

NOT ABOUT DENYING JEWISH SUFFERING

Crucially, critics of Israel's actions are not denying the reality of Jewish suffering, past or present. Many of the most prominent voices condemning Israel's actions are themselves Jewish—historians, rabbis, human rights lawyers, and ordinary citizens who feel their faith and heritage compel them to oppose oppression wherever it occurs.

This is not about denying the horror of Hamas's attacks on Israeli civilians. Rather, it is about insisting that no crime justifies the mass punishment of an entire population, half of whom are children.

THE MORAL QUESTION AT THE CENTRE

At its core, the shift in public opinion is about a basic moral question: can a modern state deliberately starve, bomb, and besiege millions of civilians and remain beyond reproach? The answer, unequivocally, is no.

Writers, artists, musicians, and actors are helping society rediscover something essential: the capacity to be horrified by suffering, even when it is politically inconvenient to say so. Their voices matter because culture shapes what societies are willing to see—and what they refuse to look away from.

A TURNING POINT?

Whether this moment will translate into political change remains to be seen. Governments still arm and fund Israel; diplomatic support remains strong in many capitals. Yet something has undeniably shifted. A growing part of the public no longer sees criticism of Israel as taboo. Instead, they see silence in the face of Gaza's destruction as the true scandal.

Artists and cultural figures have played a critical role in this transformation—not because they are moral saints, but because they dared to name what so many can now see: the horror of collective punishment, the deliberate immiseration of a people, and the urgent need for accountability.

In the end, history will judge not only what happened in Gaza, but who spoke out—and who chose to look away. For now, the tide of conscience is turning, led by those whose job, at its deepest level, has always been to make us feel, to remember, and to act.

GAZA THROUGH IRISH EYES

Echoes of Occupation and Resistance

In the rolling green landscapes and buzzing cities of Ireland, thousands of miles from the battered streets of Gaza, the suffering of the Palestinian people resonates with deep emotional and historical clarity. For many Irish people—north and south—the conflict in Gaza is not merely a distant tragedy. It is a mirror reflecting the legacies of colonialism, resistance, displacement, and identity that are etched into Ireland's own national memory.

This resonance is not new. Irish solidarity with Palestine has been decades in the making, rooted in shared experiences and shaped by evolving political consciousness. But in recent years—especially since the devastating Israeli military campaigns in Gaza, including the 2023–2024 war that claimed tens of thousands of lives—the Irish perspective has grown sharper, louder, and more unified.

COLONIAL PARALLELS: A SHARED LEGACY OF PARTITION AND OPPRESSION

Ireland's history is one of occupation, partition, and struggle. British colonial rule left indelible scars—famines, land seizures, linguistic suppression, and the systematic erosion of national identity. The 1921 partition of Ireland, imposed largely without democratic consultation, split the island and sowed division that led to decades of violence and unrest in the North.

To many Irish people, the Israeli occupation of Palestine, the forced displacement of Palestinians in 1948 (the Nakba), and the ongoing settlement expansion in the West Bank bear striking resemblances to Ireland's own colonial past. The images of walled-off communities, militarised zones, checkpoints, and apartheid-like legal systems evoke the British tactics employed in Northern Ireland, particularly during the Troubles.

This historical kinship is not just rhetorical. In interviews, Irish politicians, academics, and citizens frequently draw direct comparisons. As Sinn Féin TD John Brady put it in the Dáil (Irish parliament) in 2024, "The people of Ireland, with our long history of colonisation and resistance, instinctively understand the Palestinian struggle. We cannot turn a blind eye."

GRASSROOTS SOLIDARITY AND STREET-LEVEL MOBILISATION

Over the past decade, Irish solidarity with Palestine has evolved from symbolic gestures into robust political and social action. Irish cities—from Dublin and Belfast to Cork, Derry, Limerick and Galway—have seen pro-Palestinian marches.

Irish trade unions, student groups, artists, and civil society organisations have been particularly vocal. University College Dublin and Trinity College have seen student encampments demanding institutional divestment from Israeli-linked firms. Many Irish musicians and performers have refused to play in Israel, honouring the call for a cultural boycott under the Boycott, Divestment, and Sanctions (BDS) movement.

Irish soccer fans have also made headlines, displaying Palestinian flags at matches and chanting slogans in solidarity. During Eurovision 2024, protests erupted across Ireland over Israel's participation, with the Irish broadcaster RTÉ facing public pressure to withdraw from the event entirely.

This groundswell of support is not a fringe phenomenon. Polling conducted in 2024 found that over 70% of Irish respondents view Israel's actions in Gaza as war crimes, and over 60% support the severing of diplomatic ties with Israel if the occupation continues.

POLITICAL OUTSPOKENNESS: IRELAND'S UNIQUE ROLE IN EUROPE

Ireland has taken one of the most critical stances on Israel within the European Union. Unlike other Western nations, which often frame the issue in terms of "both sides," successive Irish governments have increasingly adopted language recognising the structural roots of Palestinian suffering.

In May 2021, the Dáil became the first EU parliament to formally declare that Israel's settlements in the West Bank constituted de facto annexation—an act in violation of international law. In 2024, the Irish government backed South Africa's genocide case against Israel at the International Court of Justice and sent a delegation to The Hague in support.

Taoiseach Simon Harris, although from the traditionally centre-right Fine Gael party, stated in 2025: "Ireland will not be complicit in the collective punishment of a people. Gaza cannot be reduced to rubble without consequences." While this drew criticism from some EU partners and pro-Israel lobbyists, it was widely applauded at home.

Sinn Féin, now the largest opposition party and a likely contender for power in the next election, has gone even further—calling for the expulsion of the Israeli ambassador and full diplomatic recognition of the State of Palestine based on the 1967 borders.

Ireland's relatively neutral geopolitical position, its lack of NATO membership, and its anti-colonial legacy afford it a unique moral authority on the world stage—one it is increasingly willing to exercise.

GAZA'S ECHO IN THE IRISH PSYCHE

The devastation in Gaza—the civilian death toll, the targeted destruction of hospitals and schools, the siege-induced famine—strikes a visceral chord in Ireland. The 1847 Great Famine, during which over a million Irish people died and another million were forced to emigrate, is a historical trauma that looms large. Seeing Palestinian children starve in Khan Younis or Rafah awakens painful national memories of abandonment and injustice.

Similarly, the systematic targeting of journalists in Gaza, particularly Irish-Palestinian journalist Hind al-Khudari, whose home was destroyed in an Israeli airstrike in 2024, has provoked outrage. Irish journalists and media outlets have become some of the most consistent international voices demanding accountability.

There is also a cultural dimension to this empathy. Irish poets, musicians, and playwrights—many of whom view art as a form of resistance—have found common cause with Palestinian counterparts. Events like the Irish-Palestinian Cultural Solidarity Week, held annually in Dublin since 2018, bring together artists who believe that storytelling is a weapon against erasure.

CHALLENGES AND CRITICISMS

Despite widespread public support, Ireland's solidarity with Gaza is not without tension. Critics argue that some expressions of support risk veering into anti-Semitic territory or that Ireland, as a small nation, risks diplomatic isolation by taking such firm stances.

Others point to inconsistencies—such as Ireland's continued trade with firms operating in illegal Israeli settlements, or the slow pace of official BDS enforcement. There are also concerns that some political factions are exploiting the issue for electoral gain without committing to concrete action once in power.

Additionally, Jewish communities in Ireland, while small, have expressed discomfort with the tone of some protests, feeling that criticism of Israeli policy sometimes spills into generalised hostility. Irish Palestinian solidarity groups have, in response, worked to make clear distinctions between anti-Zionism and antisemitism, emphasising human rights and international law as their core principles.

TOWARD A JUST PEACE: WHAT IRELAND OFFERS

While Ireland cannot unilaterally change the course of the conflict in Gaza, it can—and does—offer something powerful: moral clarity, historical empathy, and grassroots pressure.

Ireland's experience with peace processes, including the Good Friday Agreement, provides useful—if imperfect—lessons about negotiation, dignity, and the need for inclusive dialogue. While conditions in Palestine/Israel differ vastly from those in Northern

Ireland, the central lesson—that peace cannot be built on domination, humiliation, or inequality—is universal.

Irish diplomats, NGOs, and peacebuilders have quietly supported reconciliation initiatives, trauma healing, and youth dialogue programmes in both Gaza and the West Bank. Irish aid agencies like Trócaire and GOAL have maintained humanitarian operations despite overwhelming challenges.

FROM THE SHANNON TO THE SHUJAIYA

Gaza is not Ireland. The scale of destruction, the geopolitical context, and the daily reality of occupation are uniquely Palestinian. But Ireland's solidarity is not about appropriation—it is about amplification.

The Irish perspective on Gaza is shaped by an intimate understanding of how colonialism dehumanises, how resistance is criminalised, and how global powers often look the other way. It is this understanding— fused with conscience, community, and commitment—that drives Ireland's continued stand for justice in Palestine.

From murals in Derry's Bogside to candlelight vigils in Galway, the message remains clear: the people of Ireland see Gaza not as a war zone on the periphery of global affairs, but as a frontline in the shared struggle for freedom and dignity.

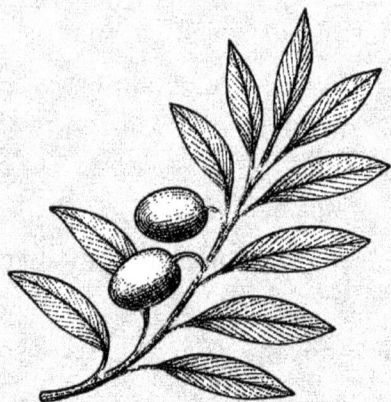

PART IV
SILENCING, MEMORY – THE BATTLE FOR NARRATIVE

GAGGING THE POETS

When Fear Mutes Verse

Poets once wielded their pens like swords, where verse erupted with the raw fire of truth and resistance, and a heavy silence now pervades. The voices that dared to speak unflinchingly about Palestine, Gaza, and the brutal realities of occupation have been systematically muted. Poetry publishers, once bastions of artistic freedom and political dissent, now retreat into the shadows of fear and caution. The pro-Palestinian political poetry that might have shaken readers awake is instead stifled, buried under layers of self-censorship and industry paranoia. This isn't just a subtle trend—it's a crisis, a cultural lockdown where fear governs what can be voiced in the lyrical space.

The crushing weight of political pressure, backlash from powerful pro-Israel lobbying groups, and the entangled relationship between American political interests and the Israeli state create a toxic atmosphere for poets and publishers alike. The fear is palpable: fear of being labelled anti-Semitic, unpatriotic, or worse, dangerous. These accusations can swiftly blacklist poets and editors, sever funding streams, and close doors once wide open for radical artistic expression. Poetry publishers, caught in this crossfire, are increasingly hesitant to take risks with politically charged material. The marketplace of ideas—once celebrated as a vibrant arena for contesting truths—has become a battleground where silence is the safer currency.

Poetry, by nature, is political. From Langston Hughes to Audre Lorde, from Mahmoud Darwish to Amiri Baraka, poets have historically been the heartbeat of resistance, chronicling the pains and hopes of oppressed peoples. Yet today, poets who write verses humanising Palestinians, mourning the children lost in Gaza's rubble, or calling out the complicity of American military aid to Israel, find themselves marginalised. Their poems are branded "too controversial" or "too risky," and are denied the platform they deserve. But this is not simply about controversy—it is about the refusal to confront inconvenient realities. These silenced voices reveal the uncomfortable truth: poetry has become a casualty in the culture wars, sacrificed at the altar of political expediency.

The censorship is insidious and often indirect. It rarely comes with official stamps or public declarations. Instead, it manifests as a creeping reticence within the publishing industry. Editors whisper about "market risks" and "audience sensitivities," invoking a language designed to police boundaries without overt confrontation. It's a form of soft censorship, a chilling effect born out of fear rather than explicit bans. This climate discourages poets from even submitting their most honest work on Palestine, let alone having it published and promoted. Publishers, juggling their survival with ethical responsibility, often choose the path of least resistance: silence.

This silence is deadly. It allows a sanitised, one-sided narrative about Gaza and Israel's military operations to dominate cultural discourse. The official framing reduces Palestinian suffering to a footnote, a collateral damage story sanitised for consumption. In this version of reality, Israel's bombings are portrayed as justified "security measures," while the voices of Palestinian poets—who speak from the rubble, the detention centres, the blockade—are erased. This erasure not only distorts history but also denies the world the essential role of poetry: to witness, to testify, and to resist.

The commercial publishing world's fear is compounded by a broader societal reluctance to engage deeply with the complexities of the Israel-Palestine conflict. In America, where political allegiance to Israel is deeply entrenched across party lines, criticism is often conflated with disloyalty or worse, bigotry. This conflation creates a poisonous environment where pro-Palestinian poetry is not just marginalised but actively feared. It threatens the carefully constructed political and cultural narratives that many institutions depend upon. The result? Poets with the courage to speak truth to power find themselves increasingly isolated, their work consigned to the margins of literary culture.

But silenced poets do not vanish. They adapt. Many are turning to independent presses, zines, online platforms, and grassroots collectives to disseminate their work. These alternative spaces, though limited in reach compared to mainstream publishers, become vital sanctuaries of resistance and creative freedom. They are the underground currents where the pulse of pro-Palestinian poetry continues to beat fiercely, reminding us that art cannot be completely contained or controlled.

This struggle to reclaim poetic voice is emblematic of a larger cultural battle—a fight against the creeping normalisation of censorship fuelled by fear and political intimidation. The stakes could not be higher. When poetry is silenced, when dissent is muted, democracy itself is weakened. Poets are not just artists; they are cultural historians, social critics, and moral witnesses. To deny them a platform is to deny society a critical mirror.

To break this silence, publishers, editors, and readers must confront their fears and their complicity. They must recognise that the true power of poetry lies in its ability to disturb, to challenge, and to humanise those whom mainstream narratives render invisible. The literary establishment must reclaim its role as a champion of fearless expression and political truth. Only then can poetry reclaim its rightful place as a weapon of resistance and a beacon of hope.

In the face of overwhelming silence, the verses that remain—those daring enough to speak—carry the weight of generations. They remind us that fear may mute the voice, but it cannot extinguish the song. The music of resistance will rise again, raw and potent, breaking through the silence, refusing to be ignored. And when it does, it will demand that we listen—truly listen—to the cries from Gaza and the calls for justice that poetry has long carried on its wings.

SHEKELS, SILENCE, AND SHACKLED SPEECH

How Western Democracies Are Losing Their Freedom

Across the democratic heartlands of the United Kingdom and the United States, a disturbing trend has emerged: the systematic suppression of pro-Palestinian protests condemning the mass violence and destruction in Gaza. Peaceful demonstrations—urgently demanding an end to what many rightly call genocide—face unprecedented legal restrictions, police intimidation, and media blackouts. This clampdown on dissent is not accidental. It unfolds amid powerful political influence wielded by foreign money from Israeli state-backed lobbyists, drowning out voices demanding justice.

Meanwhile, the erosion of freedoms of speech, assembly, and protest signals a broader crisis for democracy in these so-called liberal bastions. Yet, in this bleak landscape, Ireland stands out for its principled stance, refusing to bow to pressure and standing in solidarity with Palestinians.

THE RISING TIDE OF PRO-PALESTINIAN ACTIVISM

Since the eruption of intense conflict in Gaza, marked by relentless airstrikes, a humanitarian catastrophe, and widespread civilian deaths, millions around the world have taken to the streets to protest. These are not fringe gatherings; in major cities like London, New York, and Washington, crowds numbering in the tens of thousands have marched, demanding an immediate ceasefire and an end to Israel's military operations that have devastated Gaza.

The protests reflect widespread public concern. Polls consistently show majorities in Western countries sympathise with Palestinians' right to self-determination and oppose the violence wrought by Israeli military actions. A YouGov poll in 2024 found that 64% of Britons support calls for an immediate ceasefire in Gaza, while a Pew Research Centre survey indicated that 58% of Americans believe Israel's response has been disproportionate.

Yet, despite this groundswell of popular opposition to the violence, governments in London and Washington have responded not with empathy or dialogue but with repression.

LAWS DESIGNED TO SILENCE: THE CRIMINALISATION OF PROTEST

In the UK, the government has passed sweeping legislation that effectively criminalises protests deemed "disruptive." The Police, Crime, Sentencing and Courts Act 2022 gave police wide powers to impose conditions on protests and arrest demonstrators, even when they are peaceful. Protesters who "lock on" to structures or block roads—a common tactic to draw attention—face hefty penalties, including potential jail time.

During recent pro-Palestinian marches in London, dozens were arrested under these new laws. The police cited vague concerns about "public order" despite demonstrators peacefully exercising their democratic rights.

Similarly, in the United States, more than 40 states have enacted or proposed legislation restricting protest activities. These laws often include provisions that elevate the penalties for blocking traffic or participating in "unlawful assemblies." Some even shield drivers who hit protesters from civil or criminal liability.

The chilling effect is palpable: activists report increased police surveillance, the threat of heavy fines, and the risk of felony charges simply for standing up against genocide. As Jamil Dakwar, Director of the ACLU's Human Rights Programme, warned, "These laws are less about public safety and more about protecting the interests of those who want to silence dissent."

THE SHRINKING SPACE FOR FREE SPEECH

The suppression extends beyond the streets to the digital realm and public discourse. The UK's Online Safety Act 2023 requires tech companies to remove "legal but harmful" content, a nebulous category that critics say will likely target videos and posts critical of Israel's military campaigns or supportive of Palestinian resistance.

On social media platforms in the US, content about Gaza often faces swift removal or demonetisation. Independent journalists and activists report sudden account suspensions or censorship when exposing civilian casualties or calling for boycott campaigns.

This environment fosters self-censorship. Individuals and organisations who might otherwise speak out against genocide think twice, fearing legal repercussions or social media bans.

FOREIGN MONEY, FOREIGN INFLUENCE: HOW LOBBYING SHAPES POLICY

At the heart of this crackdown lies an undeniable reality: the influence of foreign lobbying money, much of it tied to the Israeli government and its allies, in shaping policy and silencing criticism.

In the United States, pro-Israel lobby groups such as the American Israel Public Affairs Committee (AIPAC) spend hundreds of millions annually on lobbying and campaign contributions. In the 2022 midterms alone, AIPAC's affiliated political action committees spent over $30 million backing candidates supportive of Israeli policies and opposing those critical of occupation or settlement expansion.

This financial muscle deters politicians from speaking out. Progressive US lawmakers like Representatives Ilhan Omar and Rashida Tlaib have faced vehement backlash, accusations of antisemitism, and threats simply for advocating Palestinian rights.

In the UK, groups like Labour Friends of Israel and Conservative Friends of Israel wield significant influence. While less transparent, these organisations facilitate access, campaign support, and lobbying that help maintain political consensus in favour of Israel. MPs critical of Israel's actions face pressure, isolation, and occasionally, career repercussions.

This is not about ethnic or religious identity. It is a political and financial reality where a foreign government, through its well-resourced lobby groups, shapes the discourse and policy of Western democracies—especially when that government is accused of egregious human rights violations.

WHEN CRITICISM IS BRANDED HATE

One of the most worrying aspects of this dynamic is the frequent conflation of legitimate criticism of Israel's policies with antisemitism. This conflation stifles debate and punishes those who dare question Israel's military conduct or occupation.

In the UK, for example, former Labour leader Jeremy Corbyn was subjected to intense scrutiny and eventual political exclusion amid accusations of tolerating antisemitism within his party—claims widely disputed and seen by many as politically motivated.

Similarly, in the US, criticism of Israeli policy often triggers swift condemnation and silencing efforts from both government officials and media outlets.

This creates an environment where many politicians and media personalities self-censor to avoid accusations, further shrinking the space for honest discussion about Palestinian rights and Israeli actions.

IRELAND: A BEACON OF PRINCIPLE

In stark contrast, Ireland has taken a notable stand in defence of Palestinian rights and democratic freedoms. Reflecting its history of colonisation and struggle for independence, Ireland has been unafraid to criticise Israeli policies openly. Ireland recently passed the Occupied Territories Bill, aimed at banning imports from illegal Israeli settlements in the occupied West Bank—an initiative grounded in international law. This has sent a clear message of Ireland's commitment to justice.

In 2021, the Irish parliament condemned Israeli settlement expansion as "de facto annexation," becoming the first EU legislature to do so. The then Minister of Foreign Affairs, Simon Coveney, stated: "Ireland's stance is not against Israel's right to exist but against violations of international law and human rights."

Irish civil society, too, has been active, with protests and vocal support for Palestinian rights, highlighting the fundamental connection between Ireland's own history and its support for oppressed peoples globally.

WHY THIS MATTERS TO DEMOCRACY

The erosion of protest rights and free speech on such a critical issue is a warning sign for democracy itself. Democracy thrives on open debate, dissent, and the ability of citizens to challenge their governments.

When peaceful protesters are criminalised, when speech is censored, and when foreign money shields perpetrators from criticism, democracy's core is at risk. The consequence is not only the silencing of Palestinians' plight but the undermining of democratic norms that protect all citizens.

WHAT MUST BE DONE?

The defence of democracy and human rights requires urgent, concrete action:

- **Repeal laws** that criminalise peaceful protest and impose vague restrictions on assembly.

- **Protect free speech**, ensuring that criticism of foreign governments is not censored or punished.

- **Increase transparency** in campaign finance and impose strict limits on foreign lobbying and donations.

- **Recognise the legitimacy** of pro-Palestinian activism and stop conflating criticism of Israeli policies with hate speech.

- **Support independent media and platforms** that give voice to marginalised narratives.

Only by doing so can the right to protest and speak freely be restored—and with it, the democratic promise of holding power accountable.

A MOMENT OF RECKONING

As bombs continue to fall on Gaza, and as the world watches, the actions of Western democracies speak volumes. By criminalising protest and silencing speech, the UK and USA betray the very values they claim to uphold. Foreign lobbying money acts as a buffer, protecting those responsible for atrocities from scrutiny.

Yet democracy is not lost. Ireland's example shows it is possible to stand for principle, even amid pressure. Citizens, activists, and lawmakers must demand the restoration of freedoms and a foreign policy rooted in justice, not profit.

The right to protest genocide is the right to defend humanity itself. The choice before us is stark: defend democracy and human rights, or allow them to be eroded in silence.

SILENCING THE TRUTH

Israel's Refusal to Allow International Journalists into Gaza is a
Dangerous Blow to Press Freedom and Global Accountability

In the midst of one of the most devastating conflicts in recent memory, the world's eyes are fixated on Gaza, a region ravaged by war and humanitarian catastrophe. Yet, as the violence escalates and the death toll rises, a critical barrier stands in the way of truth: Israel's persistent refusal to allow international journalists access to Gaza. It beggars belief that the world's media is not leading a hue and cry about this. This deliberate obstruction of the press is not just a denial of the right to report—it is a calculated suppression of accountability, transparency, and humanity itself.

THE CRUCIAL ROLE OF INDEPENDENT JOURNALISM IN CONFLICT ZONES

Independent journalism serves as a vital pillar of democracy and global justice, especially in war-torn regions. Journalists act as the eyes and ears of the world, documenting the realities on the ground, providing context, and amplifying the voices of those caught in the crossfire. They help transform abstract numbers and statistics into human stories that evoke empathy and urgency.

In conflict zones, where propaganda and misinformation run rampant, independent reporters provide a check on official narratives and help expose violations of international law. They bring transparency to military operations and document civilian casualties, destruction, and humanitarian crises. Without their presence, the global community is left with filtered, often sanitised versions of the truth.

214

In Gaza, a region under a blockade and frequent military assaults, the role of international journalists is even more critical. They are the bridge connecting the isolated population to the rest of the world, enabling the outside to bear witness and respond. Denying them access is tantamount to cutting Gaza off from global scrutiny and support.

A HISTORY OF MEDIA RESTRICTIONS: ISRAEL'S PATTERN OF CENSORSHIP

Israel's refusal to grant media access to Gaza is not a sudden development. It is part of a broader pattern of control and censorship that has been evident throughout the numerous conflicts in Gaza over the past two decades.

During the Gaza conflicts of 2008-09, 2012, 2014, and subsequent escalations, Israel imposed strict restrictions on journalists seeking to enter Gaza, often citing security concerns. Many reporters were denied visas, faced bureaucratic obstacles, or were restricted to controlled "media tours" heavily supervised by military escorts.

This systematic limitation on independent reporting serves multiple purposes for the Israeli government. Primarily, it enables them to control the narrative by limiting what information reaches international audiences. The official messaging often emphasises Israel's right to defend itself against attacks and minimises civilian casualties or infrastructure damage in Gaza.

This media blackout also curtails the ability of Palestinian voices— especially those of civilians—to be heard internationally. Gaza's population lives under continuous siege conditions, and their first-hand testimonies are essential to understanding the full impact of the conflict. When Israel denies journalists access, it effectively silences these voices.

THE HUMAN TOLL OF GAZA'S MEDIA BLACKOUT

At the heart of this denial is a humanitarian catastrophe unfolding behind closed doors. Gaza, home to over two million Palestinians, is one of the most densely populated places on Earth. It has endured over 15 years of a strict blockade, repeated military assaults, and severe shortages of food, water, electricity, and medical supplies.

The recent war has further compounded the tragedy. Tens of thousands of civilians—mostly women and children—have been killed or injured. Hospitals are overwhelmed, power outages are frequent, and basic services are collapsing. Entire neighbourhoods have been reduced to rubble.

Yet without independent journalists present on the ground, much of this suffering remains invisible or disputed. International media must rely heavily on local sources, social media, and reports from humanitarian organisations, which, while valuable, cannot fully replace the credibility and immediacy that on-the-ground international reporting provides.

The absence of foreign correspondents makes it easier for misinformation, exaggeration, or minimisation of the civilian toll to proliferate. It also impedes the international community's ability to mobilise timely and effective humanitarian responses.

INTERNATIONAL LAW, ACCOUNTABILITY, AND THE PRESS

International humanitarian law, including the Geneva Conventions, mandates the protection of civilians during armed conflicts and requires all parties to minimise harm to non-combatants. When these laws are violated, independent evidence and documentation are essential to support calls for accountability.

Journalists serve as watchdogs, documenting possible war crimes, disproportionate attacks, and breaches of ceasefire agreements. Their work often informs investigations by human rights organisations, international courts, and UN bodies.

By restricting media access to Gaza, Israel undermines these accountability mechanisms. It creates an environment where violations can go unchallenged and perpetrators remain unaccountable. This lack of transparency damages not only the prospects for justice but also undermines Israel's own credibility on the world stage.

The international community depends on the independent press to report facts impartially. Without such reporting, it becomes difficult for governments, international organisations, and civil society to respond appropriately to the crisis.

THE BROADER CONSEQUENCES FOR PRESS FREEDOM GLOBALLY

Israel's media restrictions in Gaza also set a dangerous precedent for press freedom worldwide. If a democratic and militarily powerful state can successfully block journalists from reporting on its military actions with little pushback, it sends a message to other governments—especially authoritarian regimes—that they too can silence inconvenient truths with impunity.

In conflict zones across the globe—from Syria to Yemen, Myanmar to Ukraine—journalists face harassment, violence, and restrictions designed to limit independent reporting. Israel's example risks normalising this behaviour and eroding global standards for press freedom.

Media organisations and journalist advocacy groups have repeatedly condemned such restrictions. The Committee to Protect Journalists (CPJ), Reporters Without Borders (RSF), and others have emphasised that access to conflict zones is essential for transparency and justice. The silencing of Gaza's story is a loss for journalism worldwide. It weakens the profession's ability to fulfil its core mission: bearing witness and holding power accountable.

THE LIMITS OF REMOTE REPORTING

Some might argue that with today's technology—smartphones, social media platforms, and satellite communications—journalists do not necessarily need physical presence in Gaza to report effectively.

While remote reporting is helpful and often necessary, it is not an adequate substitute for being on the ground. Remote sources may be vulnerable to pressure, censorship, or intimidation and may not be able to provide the same breadth and depth of information.

Physical presence allows journalists to verify facts independently, interview a diverse range of sources, and document scenes visually and contextually. It also provides a level of protection to local journalists, as international reporters can amplify their voices and offer some degree of international scrutiny that deters abuses.

Moreover, foreign correspondents can provide the world with nuanced, balanced coverage that transcends social media noise and partisan narratives.

THE MORAL AND PRACTICAL IMPERATIVE FOR CHANGE

It is incumbent upon the international community, media organisations, and governments to pressure Israel to lift its restrictions on journalists entering Gaza.

Denying media access is not just a violation of press freedom but a moral failure. The world has a right—and a responsibility—to know what is happening to Gaza's civilians. Allowing transparent reporting is a step toward safeguarding human rights, enabling effective humanitarian aid, and paving the way for accountability and peace.

Israel must recognise that press access does not undermine its security but reinforces its commitment to international norms and transparency. Mechanisms can be put in place to ensure journalists' safety while respecting operational security. This balance is standard practice in many conflict zones. The failure to permit independent reporting erodes trust, fuels resentment, and prolongs conflict. The ongoing suffering in Gaza demands that truth be told without filters or delays.

THE RIGHT TO KNOW IS A HUMAN RIGHT.

In times of war and crisis, the right to information becomes a lifeline for millions. Israel's refusal to allow international journalists into

Gaza is a calculated act of censorship that denies the world the ability to bear witness and respond to an unfolding humanitarian tragedy.

Press freedom is not a luxury or a partisan issue—it is a fundamental human right essential to justice, peace, and the protection of civilian lives. The international community must unite in demanding that Gaza be reopened to independent media immediately.

Only through transparent, courageous journalism can the suffering of Gaza's people be recognised, understood, and ultimately, addressed. Without it, the shadows of war will only deepen, and the hope for lasting peace will dim further.

SACRED JUSTIFICATIONS AND COLONIAL VIOLENCE

How Theological Narratives Serve the Notion of Israeli Supremacy

Modern colonial ideologies have often drawn on religious narratives to cloak expansionist and genocidal projects in the language of divine purpose. In the case of Israel, a settler-colonial state sustained through military occupation and systemic displacement of Palestinians, the theological infrastructure of the Old Testament has been periodically conscripted into service, not merely as a historical text; the Hebrew Bible becomes, in certain ideological currents, a living political weapon—a blueprint of conquest, retribution, and divine entitlement.

This chapter critically examines how Old Testament narratives, particularly those emphasising divine election, retributive justice, and territorial conquest, feed into the supremacist psyche that underpins the impunity of the Israeli state. By exploring how these narratives have been interpreted, co-opted, and weaponised, we expose theological scaffolding that enables war crimes and justifies apartheid under the guise of an ancient mandate.

DIVINE ELECTION AND THE CULT OF CHOSENNESS

The root of supremacist theology in Israeli ideology can be traced to Deuteronomy 7:6: *"For you are a people holy to the Lord your God; the Lord your God has chosen you out of all the peoples on the face of the earth."* This verse establishes the foundation for a divine hierarchy among nations. Although it originally functioned as a spiritual covenant, when transferred into the realm of modern nationalism, chosenness becomes exclusivism.

221

The Zionist movement, particularly in its religious manifestations, reinterprets this divine selection as political entitlement. The land is not merely a home for the persecuted; it is *rightfully and eternally theirs*, bestowed by God, regardless of the indigenous people already inhabiting it. When chosenness is coupled with state power and military might, it evolves from theological identity into imperial license.

This belief manifests most viscerally in the settler movement, where illegal outposts across the West Bank are defended as the reestablishment of biblical towns. Here, scripture is less a spiritual guide and more an ancient title deed, immune to international law or ethical scrutiny.

LEX TALIONIS AND THE LOGIC OF OVERKILL

"An eye for an eye, a tooth for a tooth" (Exodus 21:24) is often misread as a principle of proportional justice. Yet in practice, it has been used by the Israeli state as a theological and cultural precedent for collective punishment and retaliatory overreach. The Dahiya Doctrine, the Israeli military strategy advocating disproportionate force to deter future attacks, is a modern embodiment of this ethos. It systematises punishment not of perpetrators but of entire civilian populations— flattening neighbourhoods, destroying infrastructure, and inflicting mass suffering in Gaza, Lebanon, and elsewhere.

Though rabbinic Judaism historically moved away from literal retribution, the re-emergence of this ethos in state violence signals a regression: the retribalisation of justice, sanctified by historical injury and elevated to strategic necessity. The psychological resonance of perpetual victimhood—fuelled by centuries of antisemitism and the trauma of the Holocaust—feeds into a state identity that perceives every threat as existential, every retaliation as righteous.

This moral absolutism cultivates a dangerous duality: Israel sees itself as both eternal victim and divine executor of justice. In this worldview, condemnation from the international community becomes not a moral check but further evidence of persecution.

JOSHUA'S CONQUEST AND THE COLONISER'S BLUEPRINT

The Book of Joshua provides perhaps the most explicit biblical justification for genocide in the name of divine will. Canaanites are to be eradicated—not converted, not negotiated with, but utterly destroyed. *"You must destroy them totally. Make no treaty with them and show them no mercy."* (Deuteronomy 7:2)

This ethic has been internalised by elements of Israeli settler-colonial ideology. The Canaanite archetype is transposed onto the Palestinian: an inconvenient native, an obstacle to divine fulfilment. Extremist rabbis like Dov Lior and ideologues within the Religious Zionist camp have invoked such verses directly, referring to Palestinians as modern-day Amalekites—divinely marked for annihilation.

Such interpretations are not marginal. They inform policy and military strategy. They justify the erasure of Palestinian villages, the assassination of political figures, and the imprisonment of children. The conquest narrative thus functions as a theopolitical template: kill, dispossess, and claim—all under God's banner.

THE STATE AS TEMPLE: ZIONISM'S POLITICAL THEOLOGY

Secular Zionism began as a European nationalist movement, but over time, it absorbed biblical tropes to root its modern project in ancient myth. Leaders like David Ben-Gurion quoted the Bible more frequently than the Talmud, portraying the Jewish state as a resurrection of biblical Israel. In this schema, Tel Aviv becomes the new Jerusalem, the Knesset a modern Sanhedrin.

By transforming political Zionism into a sacralised movement, the Israeli state becomes more than a government—it becomes the vessel of prophecy. This sacralisation blurs the lines between spiritual aspiration and militarised entitlement. It instils the belief that criticism of Israel is not merely political dissent but blasphemy—a threat to divine will.

In such a context, the occupation of Palestinian land ceases to be a policy question; it becomes a matter of faith. International law becomes subordinate to divine right. The legal framework of the United Nations is rendered irrelevant in the face of covenantal supremacy.

IMPUNITY AS A THEOLOGICAL MANDATE

Israel's refusal to abide by international rulings—from UN resolutions to the International Court of Justice—can be seen as more than political stubbornness. It is undergirded by theological exceptionalism. If the land was promised by God, no human institution can overrule that mandate.

This impunity is reinforced by a global architecture of complicity. The U.S. veto in the Security Council, the European Union's tepid condemnations, and Arab regimes' normalisation deals create a buffer of untouchability. Within this impunity bubble, the Israeli state exercises sovereign violence with virtually no accountability.

Massacres in Jenin, sieges in Gaza, and the targeting of journalists and medics become footnotes in a liturgy of conquest. Even when evidence of war crimes is irrefutable, the sacred narrative of national survival overrides all ethical constraint.

INTERNAL RESISTANCE: JEWISH VOICES AGAINST SUPREMACY

It is essential to distinguish between Judaism and the Israeli state, between Jewish ethics and Zionist militarism. Many Jewish theologians, both within and outside Israel, fiercely reject the co-optation of scripture to justify oppression.

Movements such as Jewish Voice for Peace and T'ruah reclaim the prophetic tradition as a voice for the marginalised, not the powerful. They cite verses such as *"Justice, justice shall you pursue"* (Deuteronomy 16:20) as a counterweight to conquest theology. The Talmudic injunction that *"whoever saves a life saves the world entire"* stands in direct opposition to the logic of siege and carpet bombing.

These voices, though often sidelined, represent the ethical core of a tradition that values dissent, debate, and compassion. They remind us that Judaism, like all religions, contains multitudes—and that the divine does not speak only through generals and governments.

CHOOSING THE SACRED OR THE SACRIFICIAL

The Old Testament is a vast, contradictory archive. It contains commandments of love and tales of annihilation, visions of justice and blueprints for genocide. Which stories a nation chooses to elevate reveals not its theology but its morality.

Israel, in aligning itself with conquest narratives and chosenness myths, has constructed a self-image that sacralises violence and erases its victims. The result is a state that operates with theological impunity, cloaking modern war crimes in ancient righteousness.

To break this cycle, a desacralisation of the state is necessary. Scripture must be returned to the realm of moral inquiry, not geopolitical strategy. Until then, the divine will continue to be weaponised, not to uplift the oppressed, but to sanctify the machinery of oppression itself.

This chapter is not a condemnation of Judaism, but a call to rescue it from the grip of nationalist theology. It is a challenge to reclaim the sacred from the sacrificial, to choose justice over justification, and to tell new stories—stories where no one must die to prove divine favour.

REWRITING THE NARRATIVE

In reckoning with the violence made possible by misapplied sacred texts, it becomes clear that the Old Testament is not unique in its vulnerability to misuse. Just as Christian colonial powers once baptised slavery, genocide, and empire, and just as Islamic extremists have distorted jihad into indiscriminate violence, Zionist statecraft has selectively weaponised scripture to build walls—literal and theological—between justice and power.

But there remains another way to read these texts. The prophets of the Hebrew Bible—Isaiah, Amos, Micah—railed against injustice, called out kings, and defended the widow, the orphan, and the stranger. This counter-narrative has been buried under rubble and rhetoric, but it has not disappeared. It is carried forward by those within and beyond the Jewish community who refuse to sanctify apartheid, who speak for peace with dignity, and who seek solidarity over supremacy.

Deconstructing the sacred justifications for Israeli state violence is not an attack on Judaism but a defence of it—of its capacity for moral renewal and prophetic witness. The task ahead is not only political resistance but hermeneutic resistance: to interpret differently, to resist theologies of death, and to recover from the ashes of divine wrath a flame of human dignity.

We must remember that sacred texts are not shackles but mirrors. What we find in them depends on what we bring to them. If we search only for conquest, we will find it. If we search for justice, mercy, and peace, they too are waiting to be revealed.

BLIND FAITH AND BLIND POLITICS

How American Evangelicals Chose Power Over Principle in Israel-Palestine[3]

In the long, anguished history of the Holy Land, few forces have proved as corrosive to the hope of peace as the unwavering, often unthinking support of American evangelicals for the state of Israel. While millions speak of "standing with Israel" as if it were a pure act of faith, this solidarity too often reveals itself as political idolatry — a devotion not to justice, peace, or the teachings of Christ, but to an eschatological script and a culture war mentality that demands enemies.

This is not a new story, but it is a story that grows darker each year. Decade after decade, the evangelical community's zeal has hardened into a moral blindness, where the pursuit of biblical prophecy and right-wing geopolitics override the cries of the oppressed and the inconvenient demands of truth. As bombs fall, walls rise, and young Palestinians see their futures shrink to rubble and razor wire, America's evangelical bloc cheers from afar, declaring the suffering necessary, even righteous. And in that cheer, they betray the very gospel they profess to uphold.

A FAITH CAPTURED BY POLITICS

To understand how this came to pass, one must see beyond the comforting myth that evangelical support for Israel is simply an

---

[3] And many (most) evangelical communities world-wide share the same theological perspective.

expression of biblical solidarity. It is, rather, a modern political construction — a marriage of dispensationalist theology, Cold War politics, and American exceptionalism.

In the 1970s and 1980s, figures like Jerry Falwell, Pat Robertson, and later John Hagee infused evangelical culture with a fervent Christian Zionism. They preached that the return of Jews to the land of Israel was not merely a political fact but a divine mandate — the prelude to Armageddon, the Second Coming, and ultimately, the triumph of their particular brand of faith.

Yet beneath the surface of prophecy lay an all-too-human desire: to wield power. Supporting Israel became a badge of belonging within the Republican coalition, a signal of unwavering commitment to a black-and-white moral universe in which the West (and Israel) embodied goodness, and their enemies embodied evil. Over time, the spiritual dimension became inextricable from a nationalist impulse: evangelicals would "bless" Israel not merely for heaven's reward but to wage their own culture wars on earth.

In this alliance, faith became fused with force. And so a community whose founder preached "blessed are the peacemakers" became the most reliable American constituency cheering every new settlement, every wall, every bomb dropped on Gaza — all in the name of biblical fidelity.

A THEOLOGY OF SACRIFICE — BUT NOT THEIR OWN

What makes this position so devastating is not just its effect on policy, but the underlying moral calculus: American evangelicals, many of whom have never set foot in the Middle East, sanctify violence and

229

dispossession inflicted on other people, so long as it fits the script they believe God has written.

Consider the logic: Palestinian displacement becomes a "sign of the times," evidence that prophecy is unfolding; Israeli military actions are seen not as human choices subject to moral scrutiny, but as steps foreordained by divine will. The victims — civilians killed in bombings, children in refugee camps, families evicted from ancestral homes — become props, their suffering explained away or rendered invisible.

This is a theology of sacrifice, but always someone else's sacrifice. It is easy to bless a war when you will never hear the sirens or bury the dead. It is easy to call for unending confrontation when you imagine that confrontation must precede the final glory of your own salvation.

SILENCE ON JUSTICE AND WORSE

The result is not merely theological distortion, but moral abdication. The evangelical establishment often insists it loves "the Jewish people" — and perhaps it does, in a selective, utilitarian way — yet it expresses a chilling indifference to actual justice and peace.

When Israeli politicians expand settlements in blatant violation of international law, evangelicals do not protest. When Israeli forces kill journalists or peaceful demonstrators, they remain silent. When Christian Palestinians (the oldest Christian communities in the world) cry out against occupation and discrimination, American evangelicals turn their backs.

It is a silence that reveals a terrible truth: for too many, justice is irrelevant unless it advances the end-times narrative. Peace is undesirable if it delays prophecy. Truth is inconvenient if it complicates the story they have chosen to believe.

THE GOSPEL BETRAYED

In embracing this political idolatry, evangelicals have not merely failed their Palestinian neighbours; they have betrayed the radical, unsettling message of the gospel itself.

At the heart of Christian teaching is the idea that every person, every community, bears the image of God and demands dignity. Christ stood with the oppressed and called his followers to do the same, even when it was costly. He blessed the peacemakers, not the warmongers. He wept for cities doomed by violence.

Yet in the evangelical discourse on Israel, the humanity of Palestinians vanishes almost entirely. They become a faceless mass, either obstacles to prophecy or foot soldiers of radical Islam. Their legitimate grievances — exile, occupation, statelessness — are waved away. Even Palestinian Christians are often accused of heresy if they challenge the narrative.

What remains is not faith but a simulacrum: a brittle, triumphalist ideology that dresses itself in scripture but is rooted in fear, pride, and tribal loyalty.

THE COST AND THE OPPORTUNITY LOST.

The practical costs are enormous. American evangelicals wield significant political influence, and their uncritical support has helped sustain decades of **U.S.** policy that shields Israel from accountability while starving diplomatic efforts for peace.

Yet the deeper tragedy is spiritual. Imagine if that same energy, money, and passion were directed toward reconciliation rather than endless conflict. Imagine evangelical churches supporting coexistence projects, building schools and hospitals in both Israel and Palestine, demanding justice for all people of the land rather than just one side.

Such a movement could have been a prophetic witness: a voice refusing to be captive to any state or ideology, insisting that peace is possible and necessary. Instead, evangelicals largely chose to be court prophets, baptising the status quo in holy language.

A CRISIS OF WITNESS

There are, of course, exceptions. A growing minority of evangelicals are challenging the old orthodoxy, travelling to the region, listening to Palestinian Christians, and questioning the dogmas of Christian Zionism. But they remain marginalised, often dismissed as naïve or even anti-Semitic for daring to ask whether justice should be universal rather than selective.

This moment, then, is a crisis of witness: will American evangelicals remain known as cheerleaders of power and occupation, or can they recover a faith rooted in compassion, truth, and humility?

For decades, evangelical leaders have warned of the danger of moral relativism in secular society. Yet they have practised their own form of moral relativism: condemning violence when it suits them, blessing it when it serves prophecy; defending human rights in abstract but rejecting them when they complicate loyalty to Israel.

What is missing is not knowledge — the facts of occupation, displacement, and suffering are well documented — but courage, the courage to see the other as fully human, the courage to break from tribal loyalty. The courage to believe that God is not a nationalist and that faith does not demand blindness.

TOWARD A NEW WITNESS

If American evangelicals are to have any credible moral voice in the future, it must begin with repentance: an honest reckoning with decades of complicity in injustice. It must mean listening to Palestinian Christians, recognising the daily indignities and violence of occupation, and refusing to see any human being as expendable for the sake of prophecy.

It must mean rejecting the seductive myth that God's purposes depend on tanks, walls, and bombs, and remembering instead the Jesus who entered Jerusalem on a donkey, wept for the city, and offered peace.

It must mean recovering the ancient truth that peace-making is holy work, even when it is slow and imperfect. That justice must be impartial, or it is no justice at all. That faith is not proven by the ability to demonise the other, but by the willingness to love them.

The story of American evangelicals and Israel is not yet finished. But it is at a turning point. The question is not whether Christians should care about Israel — of course they should — but whether they will care about Palestinians too. Whether they will choose prophecy over people, or remember that faith demands seeing the face of Christ in every neighbour, even the inconvenient ones.

In the end, what is at stake is not just the fate of a distant land, but the integrity of the evangelical witness itself. For what shall it profit a movement to gain political influence, yet lose its soul?

233

THE NAKBA NEVER ENDED

Narratives of Memory, Trauma, and Resistance

The war on Gaza today has left tens of thousands of Palestinians dead—most of them civilians, many of them women and children. Entire neighbourhoods lie in ruins, hospitals are reduced to rubble, and hundreds of thousands are displaced yet again. This devastation is not an isolated tragedy, beginning with the brutality of Hamas attacks on October 7, 2023. It is the latest chapter in a much longer history that began in 1948 with the Nakba—Arabic for "catastrophe"—when over 700,000 Palestinians, about half of the pre-war Arab population, were expelled or fled from their homes during the creation of Israel.

For Palestinians, the Nakba is not a historical event locked in the past. It is an ongoing reality. It lives in refugee camps across the Middle East, in the occupied territories, and most painfully, in Gaza—the world's largest open-air prison. Each new assault is layered upon decades of dispossession, siege, and erasure. The trauma is sustained, transmitted, and inherited. What is happening now is not a break from the past. It is its continuation.

A CATASTROPHE WITH NO END

Nakba Day is commemorated each year on May 15, the day after Israeli Independence Day (Yom Ha'atzmaut). Instituted by Yasser Arafat in 1998, it marks not only the initial catastrophe of 1948 but also the persistence of loss and exile. For Israelis, it is a day of celebration; for Palestinians, a day of mourning. Like the contentious Twelfth of July marches in Northern Ireland, one group's celebration is another's wound.

Western narratives often frame the Nakba as a closed historical episode, a grim milestone to be studied in the past tense. But for Palestinians, it is ongoing. In refugee camps in Lebanon, Syria, and Jordan; in the occupied West Bank and East Jerusalem; and in Gaza—trauma is lived daily. Generations grow up not only without homes but with the enduring knowledge that the catastrophe that expelled their grandparents remains unresolved.

The Nakba was not only about land; it was about erasure. Villages were destroyed or renamed, orchards uprooted, maps redrawn. The forced transfer of millions was not just about clearing space for new settlements but also about erasing memory. Palestinians became refugees in their own homeland, and those who remained faced systematic efforts to redefine them as "good Arabs" or "Israeli Arabs," identities designed by the state to fragment and neutralise.

MEMORY AS SURVIVAL AND RESISTANCE

Memory is central to Palestinian life. Like the Irish experience of colonialism, where stories of repression shaped national consciousness, Palestinians preserve their history through oral traditions, poetry, song, and art. These are not passive recollections, but living archives of identity and resistance.

Grandmothers in refugee camps recount stories of orchards, harvests, weddings, and villages erased by war. These memories are not abstractions; they are maps of belonging, ensuring that even children born in exile know where they come from. Storytelling clarifies loss, but also affirms endurance. It transforms trauma into a shared identity project, enriching connections across generations and communities.

235

The dialectic of remembering and forgetting is one familiar to Irish history, particularly the Troubles. Just as the stories of Bloody Sunday or Ballymurphy shaped Irish republican consciousness, so too do Nakba stories shape Palestinian identity. Narratives of bravery, resilience, and dispossession offer young generations ways of connecting their present exclusion to a past rich with personal and collective detail.

Israel has long sought to erase Palestinian memory through education, censorship, and cultural suppression—Hebraizing place names, banning Nakba commemorations, and imposing curricula that omit Palestinian history. For Palestinian children, the classroom often mirrors that of colonised Irish children, who were once taught only the conqueror's version of events. Against this, the stories of mothers and grandmothers function as counter-history, instilling dignity and belonging.

CULTURAL GENOCIDE AND THE WAR ON IDENTITY

The war on Gaza is not only a military campaign—it is a cultural one. Libraries, mosques, and churches are destroyed. Universities, theatres, art galleries, and hospitals bear scars of bombardment. This is not incidental but systematic: an effort to strip Palestinians of their cultural memory and replace it with silence.

In Israel itself, Palestinian citizens are subjected to curricula that omit their past and portray their identity only in terms acceptable to the state. The "Israeli-Arab" is the identity Israel prefers, not Palestinian. Language, history, and geography are reshaped to erase the memory of a non-Jewish past. Just as Irish schoolchildren once sat in classrooms where their own history was absent or twisted, so too do Palestinian children today.

Despite these efforts, Palestinian culture has survived beneath rubble and exile. Mahmoud Darwish's poetry, folk songs recounting lost villages and new verses born from each wave of tragedy all serve as both memory and defiance. Music, painting, and drama embody resistance. They articulate grief, longing, and determination to survive. They affirm connection to land and community when both are under constant threat. Just as colonisers once sang of triumphs, Palestinians sing of return and steadfastness, refusing to let memory die.

WOMEN AS GUARDIANS OF MEMORY

Women—especially mothers and grandmothers—are the primary custodians of Palestinian history. In kitchens and courtyards, over bread-making or coffee, they pass down memories of displacement and resilience. These stories construct identity, binding personal memory to collective struggle. In the absence of textbooks, oral testimony becomes the most trusted archive.

Children raised in exile often know the layout of ancestral homes, the scent of fig trees, or the rhythm of harvests—details preserved in oral tradition. This intergenerational storytelling bridges past and present, turning personal trauma into communal belonging. These are not nostalgic recollections but deliberate acts of cultural survival.

Such stories often differentiate between "victim" and "survivor" narratives. Victim stories emphasise the loss, grief, and injustices endured. Survivor stories emphasise resilience and resistance. Both matter. Both are woven into the collective identity, reminding young Palestinians that theirs is a history not only of dispossession but also of endurance.

The role of women as guardians of memory is not only domestic but political. By keeping alive the names of villages, the rhythms of harvests, and the sounds of weddings, they resist the state's attempt to erase them. Through narrative, women secure continuity and prepare future generations to bear witness.

THE EMOTIONAL ARCHITECTURE OF EXILE

Exile is not simply a loss of place but a rupture of community and identity. The destroyed Palestinian village represents not just buildings, but kinship networks, shared celebrations, and cultural rhythms. When villages are erased, a part of the self is erased too.

This loss is not confined to one generation. Trauma is inherited, shaping the psyche of grandchildren as much as those who lived the original catastrophe. Exile manifests in emotional as well as material ways. The destroyed orchard is not just **an** economic loss but emotional devastation. The lost threshing floor or water well represents a fracture in social life and memory. These voids ripple across generations, embedding themselves in the Palestinian psyche.

The emotional impact of exile is tied to the shattering of social and cultural integration: kinship networks, economic security, shared rituals. When these are lost, people experience not only displacement but disorientation. Yet Palestinians have adapted resourcefully, building new forms of social solidarity and cultural expression even in camps and under siege.

ART, POETRY, AND THE SPIRIT OF RESISTANCE

Art in Palestine is not separate from the struggle—it is the struggle. Poetry, music, painting, and performance all serve as vehicles for expressing pain, hope, and defiance. The works of poets like Mahmoud Darwish and Fadwa Tuqan remain etched in the national consciousness, offering both balm and fire.

Palestinian folk songs—many composed in the aftermath of the Nakba—continue to evolve, incorporating new verses for each new atrocity. They are sung at funerals, weddings, and protests. They speak of land, of longing, of steadfastness. As in other colonised cultures, Palestinian art does not merely reflect life under occupation—it actively resists it. Through words, melodies, and imagery, memory is preserved, even when villages are reduced to rubble.

Folk poetry recounts not only dispossession but also continuity: the olive tree that endures, the stone house remembered, the neighbour's laughter recalled. These verses are sung not just to mourn but to resist—to insist on belonging even when belonging is denied.

A PEOPLE REFUSING ERASURE

Despite unimaginable adversity, Palestinians continue to assert their presence. They plant olive trees even as bulldozers approach. They teach their children Arabic, commemorate the Nakba every May 15, and create art and literature that defy silence. Even amid bombardment, people marry, sing lullabies, and write poetry. Such acts of everyday life are also acts of resistance.

Palestinians are often portrayed in the media as either victims or militants, rarely as thinkers, teachers, artists, or historians. But the reality is richer. They are keeping memory alive not as nostalgia, but as political defiance. They are building lives amid wreckage. They are asserting a right to exist—on their terms.

In this way, Palestinians embody what one scholar calls the "politics of steadfastness." Their survival itself, their insistence on narrating their own story, is a refusal of erasure.

THE WAR ON TRUTH

One of the most insidious aspects of the conflict is the global war on Palestinian truth. Social media platforms silence Palestinian voices. Western governments, while invoking human rights elsewhere, parrot narratives that ignore or diminish Palestinian suffering. Journalists are killed. Academics are blacklisted. The attempt is not just to destroy homes, but to destroy the very language to describe that destruction. Yet the stories keep coming. From mobile phones, from diaspora communities, from the ruins of Nuseirat and Khan Younis, Palestinians continue to speak. Their words are raw, vivid, and necessary. Memory is transmitted not only orally but digitally, ensuring that even in the face of censorship, the world continues to hear.

WHAT MUST BE REMEMBERED?

The Nakba was never a single event; it is an ongoing process of displacement, erasure, and resistance. To remember the Nakba is not only to look back, but to recognise its continuity in the present. It is to acknowledge a people's refusal to vanish, and their insistence on return, dignity, and freedom.

To commemorate the Nakba is not merely to recall tragedy. It is to affirm the persistence of a people. It is to understand that Palestinians do not seek vengeance but the right to return, to belong, to live freely on their land.

Palestine lives in stories, in songs, in the stubborn resilience of its people. Until there is justice, the Nakba continues.

Structural Psychopathy

A Psychoanalytical Portrait of Israeli State Violence and Empathy Collapse

The Gaza Strip is more than a geopolitical flashpoint; it is the epicentre of a decades-long humanitarian catastrophe fuelled by systemic policies of siege, displacement, and destruction. While international discourse often frames the Israeli-Palestinian conflict in political or military terms, it is imperative to examine the psychological mechanisms underpinning such sustained and normalised violence. Through the lens of psychoanalysis and political psychology, we must confront a deeply disturbing pattern: the Israeli state's behaviour toward Palestinians, particularly in Gaza, displays traits that reflect a structural and institutional psychopathy — an emotional and moral detachment from human suffering, embedded within the state apparatus and echoed in its society.

This is not a careless application of clinical language. Psychopathy, in its clinical sense, refers to a specific constellation of traits including lack of empathy, remorselessness, manipulativeness, and a propensity for calculated cruelty. While it would be irresponsible to diagnose a collective with a condition designed for individuals, it is psychologically valid to discuss the *structural analogues* of psychopathy as they manifest in state policy, military strategy, public narratives, and societal attitudes. In this context, Israel's treatment of Palestinians can be examined as a form of state-level empathy erosion and moral disengagement that aligns disturbingly with these psychopathic patterns.

Since 2007, Israel has enforced a comprehensive blockade on the Gaza Strip, effectively sealing off a population of over two million people from the rest of the world. This blockade has devastated Gaza's economy, destroyed its healthcare infrastructure, and created a situation where access to clean water, electricity, medicine, and basic nutrition is erratic at best and deliberately restricted at worst. United Nations reports, as well as documentation from Human Rights Watch, Amnesty International, and the International Committee of the Red Cross, have all described the blockade as a form of collective punishment — a violation of international law.

Repeated military campaigns have only compounded the suffering. Israel's operations in Gaza have resulted in the deaths of thousands of civilians, many of them children. Whole neighbourhoods have been flattened, schools, hospitals, and UN shelters have been bombed. In the aftermath of these assaults, the Israeli government has consistently justified its actions using the language of self-defence, framing all Palestinian casualties as collateral damage or the consequence of Hamas' alleged use of human shields. This rhetorical framework allows for the systematic erasure of Palestinian personhood. The death of a child becomes not a tragedy but a regrettable strategic mishap. The flattening of a home is not violence but a neutralised threat. These narratives strip Palestinians of individual identity and agency, reducing them to functions in a military calculus.

From a psychological perspective, this is a textbook case of dehumanisation. Dehumanisation is a cognitive and emotional process by which the perceived humanity of the other is denied, thereby lowering the threshold for cruelty. It is a prerequisite for atrocity. In the Israeli case, the dehumanisation of Palestinians is not only practised at the level of military strategy but is reinforced through media, political discourse, and public education. Palestinians are frequently portrayed in Israeli media as inherently violent, irrational, or complicit in terrorism. This produces what psychologists call "empathy fatigue" — a condition where the suffering of the out-group no longer registers as morally significant.

This empathy collapse is further entrenched by Israel's national identity narrative. The legacy of the Holocaust and the history of Jewish persecution are central to the Israeli state's founding ethos. These historical traumas, while legitimate and profound, have been instrumentalised into a form of permanent existential anxiety — the belief that the Jewish people are always under threat and must respond with uncompromising force. When trauma is not metabolised but instead encoded into state identity, it creates a closed circuit of justification. All actions, no matter how extreme, become permissible under the logic of survival. This is what psychoanalyst Vamik Volkan refers to as "chosen trauma": the recycling of historical wounds as the basis for present-day aggression.

The implications of this are profound. A society that defines itself through unprocessed trauma can project that trauma outward, transforming from victim to aggressor while maintaining a self-image of righteousness. This inversion enables what psychologists call moral disengagement — the process by which individuals or groups rationalise harmful behaviour by disassociating it from ethical norms. In Israel, moral disengagement is institutionalised. The suffering of Palestinians is reframed as their own fault, the result of their leadership, their resistance, their culture. This is a hallmark of psychopathic reasoning: the denial of accountability and the redirection of blame onto the victim.

Public opinion within Israel reflects and reinforces these pathologies. Numerous surveys during and after military operations show high levels of support among Israeli citizens for campaigns that result in massive civilian casualties. These are not fringe views. They represent a societal consensus shaped by decades of indoctrination, militarisation, and fear. Critics within Israeli society, including Jewish scholars and activists who speak out against these policies, are routinely marginalised, smeared, or accused of treason. This silencing of dissent is not just political control; it is psychological closure. It is the refusal to tolerate empathy because empathy threatens the ideological armour.

The psychological profile of Israel's state behaviour, therefore, aligns with what can be called structural psychopathy. This is not about individual malice. It is about a system in which emotional detachment, rationalised cruelty, and moral inversion are built into the very architecture of governance and public consciousness. The state does not feel guilt. It does not change course in the face of atrocity. It doubles down. It escalates. It denies. It explains. It moves on.

In psychoanalytic terms, this reflects a profound narcissistic wound — a collective ego that cannot integrate the idea of wrongdoing without collapsing. Instead of introspection, it reacts with rage, projection, and violence. The international community, when it criticises Israel, is labelled anti-Semitic. Human rights observers are dismissed as biased. Palestinian voices are excluded entirely. This is the psychology of a system that has lost the capacity for self-reflection and remorse.

None of this analysis negates the legitimate fears and traumas that many Israelis carry. But those fears cannot justify the starvation of civilians, the bombing of hospitals, and the killing of children. Trauma must not become a license. If anything, people who have suffered deeply should be the most sensitive to the suffering of others. Instead, we witness the opposite: a national policy apparatus that treats empathy as a liability.

The international community has largely failed to confront this structural psychopathy with the seriousness it demands. Statements of concern, resolutions without enforcement, and selective outrage have enabled the continuation of these policies. The silence or complicity of Western governments, particularly the United States, only deepens the moral vacuum. What is needed is not more equivocation but a clear and unflinching confrontation with the psychological and ethical reality of what is taking place.

The world must name what it sees. This is not just a military conflict. It is a sustained campaign of dehumanisation and control executed with cold emotional detachment and justified through a self-righteous national mythos. It is cruelty without remorse. It is violence without limits. It is structural psychopathy.

If the arc of the moral universe is to bend toward justice, then it must also bend toward psychological clarity. We must ask: what kind of society supports this? What kind of state justifies this? What kind of world allows it to continue?

The answers are difficult, but they are necessary. To ignore them is to abdicate not only political responsibility but our shared humanity. It is to become part of the pathology. It is to watch suffering and do nothing. It is, in the final analysis, a failure not just of politics but of empathy itself.

SILENCE THEN AND NOW

What Gaza Reveals About Who We Really Are

Have you ever truly stopped to wonder what choices you might have made as an adult living in Nazi Germany between 1936 and 1945? Would you have stood against a monstrous ideology rooted in hate, violence, and dehumanisation? Would you have dared to speak up, knowing that your dissent could cost you your freedom—or even your life? Or would fear, apathy, or the comfort of your own position have kept you quiet? Would you have pleaded ignorance, claiming you didn't know what was happening? Would you have shrugged and said, "I'm not political," or told yourself that the Nazi regime was simply too powerful to challenge?

It's a question that haunts us because it strips us of comforting illusions. We like to imagine ourselves as brave, principled, and moral people who would have risked something to do what's right. But history is rarely shaped by what we imagine we would do. It is shaped by what we actually do when faced with injustice. And today, you don't have to wonder anymore.

Look to Gaza. Look at what is happening to the Palestinian people: entire families wiped out in moments, entire neighbourhoods reduced to rubble, children pulled mutilated or lifeless from the debris, hospitals and schools destroyed, a population trapped with nowhere safe to go. It is a horror that unfolds in real time, streamed onto our screens, reported by journalists, and documented by human rights organisations. The facts are there for anyone willing to look, yet so many remain silent. And by your silence, you have your answer: this is what you would have done back then.

We often talk about historical atrocities as if they belong to some distant, unimaginable past—as if people then were somehow different from us. We assume that, had we lived under Nazi rule, we would have seen through the propaganda, recognised evil for what it was, and risked something—anything-to resist. But this assumption ignores a painful truth: people living through those years were not so different. They, too, had families, jobs, fears, and ambitions. They, too, feared consequences, arrest, social ostracism, and violence. Many, perhaps most, turned away not because they were fanatical Nazis, but because they felt powerless or told themselves it wasn't their responsibility.

Today, the situation in Gaza forces us to confront that same moral test, but without the excuses of distance or ignorance. In the age of instant communication and global media, we can no longer claim "I didn't know." We see it, read it, hear it. And still, many of us remain silent.

To say, "I'm not political," is to echo the words of countless bystanders in history. To say, "It's too complicated," is to look away from suffering because it unsettles us. To say, "What can I do?" is to choose helplessness over responsibility. Each of these choices is, in effect, a decision to do nothing—and doing nothing is a decision with consequences.

THE MYTH OF NEUTRALITY

Neutrality in the face of injustice isn't moral. It isn't compassionate. It isn't even truly neutral. It's complicity. When an atrocity is happening, there is no balanced middle ground between the oppressed and the oppressor. Refusing to speak out doesn't absolve you; it empowers those committing the violence. Silence tells the perpetrators: the world is watching—and the world does not care enough to stop us.

History makes this painfully clear. The Nazi regime was enabled not just by fervent supporters, but by the millions who looked away, who insisted they were "just trying to live their lives," who said nothing as their Jewish neighbours disappeared.

In South Africa, apartheid survived for decades not only because of its enforcers but because of those around the world who accepted trade, travel, and polite diplomatic relations instead of demanding an end to racial terror.

In the American South, segregation persisted because so many white citizens refused to challenge it—even if they claimed, privately, to disagree.

In each case, the silence of ordinary people played an active role in sustaining the machinery of oppression.

FEAR AND SELF-INTEREST – POWERFUL INCENTIVES TO STAY SILENT

Let's be honest: there are real reasons why people remain silent. Some fear backlash—from employers, friends, or family. Some worry about being labelled, attacked online, or losing social standing. Others fear feeling powerless, believing that a single voice means nothing against the might of states and armies.

But these are the same fears that shaped the choices of millions before us. Fear of "consequences" isn't new. It's what kept so many people in Nazi Germany silent while their Jewish neighbours were rounded up. It's what kept so many white Americans silent during the lynching era, knowing that to speak out meant to risk ostracism or violence. And it is what keeps many silent today as Palestinian lives are extinguished.

The truth is that silence has consequences, too—not just for the victims of oppression, but for us. It corrodes our moral sense, teaching us to live comfortably alongside horror. It makes us smaller, colder, and ultimately complicit.

THE POWER OF A SINGLE VOICE

It's easy to dismiss our individual voices as insignificant. But history is full of moments when the courage of even a few people made a difference—when a letter to a newspaper, a protest sign, or a conversation changed minds and built momentum for change.

We don't need to be famous activists or politicians to matter. Speaking out—on social media, in conversation, in our communities—can shift what is seen as normal, what is seen as acceptable. It sends a message to those in power: people are watching, people do care, and people will remember. We may not be able to stop bombs from falling. But we can refuse to be silent as they do.

WORDS ALONE ARE NOT ENOUGH—BUT SILENCE IS WORSE.

Some will say: "Talking isn't enough." And they're right. Real change requires action: donating to humanitarian aid, lobbying politicians, protesting, boycotting and educating others. But silence ensures nothing changes at all. Silence kills empathy, buries truth, and shields injustice.

We can't allow the enormity of the problem to paralyse us. Instead, we must see it as a call to act—to do what we can, where we can, even if it feels small.

THE COST OF LOOKING AWAY

History will judge us, as it judges all generations. And when it does, it will not be kind to our excuses. Already, children in Gaza are growing up under unimaginable trauma—or not growing up at all. Families mourn loved ones buried under rubble. And as they do, the world debates language, questions definitions, and turns away.

In decades to come, people will ask what we did—what we said—while this happened. They won't ask what we felt in our hearts. They will ask what we did with our voices, our votes, our platforms, and our privilege.

To say "I was not political" or "I was afraid of consequences" will not sound noble. It will sound hollow. It will sound like what it is: complicity.

A MIRROR TO OURSELVES

When we ask, "What would I have done in Nazi Germany?" or "What would I have done during segregation?" the answer isn't in our imagination. It's in our actions today. Are we willing to raise our voices, risk discomfort, challenge our circles, and reject the comfort of neutrality? Or do we look away, hoping someone braver will do it for us? If your answer today is silence, then you have your answer to that question of history. You would have been silent then, too.

This is not about being perfect. It's about refusing to let fear and convenience silence us. It's about recognising that silence isn't neutral—it's a choice. And it's a choice that, once made, cannot be undone. Speak up—even if your voice trembles. Refuse to let horror be normalised. Refuse to be a bystander, because history is not written only by those in power. It is also written by those who stayed silent— and by those who refused to.

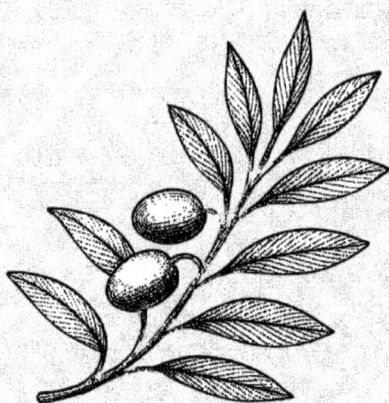

Conclusion
Beyond Silence

History will judge us not only for what we have done, but for what we have chosen to ignore. Gaza today is not simply a humanitarian tragedy born of natural disaster or accident of fate. It is a political catastrophe built over decades of occupation, dispossession, blockade, and global complicity — a catastrophe whose origins trace back through the Nakba of 1948 and the 1967 occupation, and even further to the Balfour Declaration of 1917: a colonial promise that helped set in motion a century of displacement and contested sovereignty, privileging one people's national aspirations while ignoring the rights of those already living in the land.

This book began with the idea that silence itself is not neutral. In the face of massive civilian suffering, systematic destruction, and credible accusations of crimes against humanity, silence becomes a moral choice — a choice that aligns us, whether we admit it or not, with power rather than with the powerless. "Never again," we have been taught to say; yet as bombs fell on hospitals, refugee camps, and residential towers in Gaza, many of the world's most powerful governments offered either muted regret or full-throated justification. In doing so, they made "never again" sound hollow.

The suffering in Gaza is not new. It did not begin on October 7, 2023, or even in 2007 when the blockade tightened after Hamas took power. It has roots stretching back through the 1967 occupation and the 1948 Nakba, when hundreds of thousands of Palestinians were expelled or fled their homes, becoming refugees whose descendants now make up the majority of Gaza's population. The "conflict" is often narrated as a series of wars and ceasefires, yet from Gaza's perspective, it is an unbroken chain of siege, displacement, and recurring devastation, punctuated by brief and fragile truces.

What makes the current moment so stark, however, is the combination of scale and visibility. Tens of thousands of civilians killed and injured; health systems collapsed; children buried under rubble as the world watches in real time on social media. In earlier decades, journalists might have struggled to document war crimes or show evidence quickly. Today, Palestinian journalists, doctors, and ordinary citizens broadcast live to the world, forcing us to see what once could be hidden. And yet, even in the face of such overwhelming testimony, political and media institutions often find ways to explain away the horror, blame the victims, or simply move on.

This contradiction — the immediacy of truth colliding with the durability of denial — is one of the defining features of what we have called the "genocide in a digital age." On screens across the globe, the suffering of Gaza is impossible to ignore, but in official discourse, it remains somehow invisible, unspeakable, or framed as unfortunate but necessary. Here, narrative becomes as much a weapon as artillery: through selective language, context-stripping, and the myth of "self-defence" stretched beyond legal meaning, mass civilian deaths are made politically palatable.

One of the hardest truths to confront is the role of complicity, not just by states but by all of us who benefit, directly or indirectly, from systems of power that enable injustice. The United States provides billions in military aid, with weapons traceable to the destruction of homes and schools. The European Union, while occasionally voicing "concern," trades with Israel on favourable terms and hesitates to use real leverage. Western democracies enact laws and social pressures that silence pro-Palestinian voices, from poets to professors. Meanwhile, faith-based movements like Christian Zionism sustain unconditional support for policies that deepen Palestinian suffering, often in the name of prophecy rather than peace.

To speak of genocide is never a claim to be made lightly. But when we see a besieged population, half of them children, deprived of food, water, medicine, and fuel, while bombs fall on hospitals and refugee camps; when we hear rhetoric describing an entire people as "human animals" or "no innocents," and calls to flatten entire districts; when scholars and legal experts warn that the scale and intent appear to meet the definition under international law — then we must ask: if not now, when? The point is not to cheapen the term "genocide," but to uphold its very purpose: preventing mass atrocity by naming it before it becomes history.

Justice cannot come from courts alone, though international legal processes remain crucial. The International Court of Justice (ICJ) has already issued provisional measures ordering Israel to prevent genocidal acts, though implementation is lacking. The International Criminal Court (ICC) faces intense political pressure to delay or soften investigations. Legal accountability matters, but so does moral accountability: an insistence by citizens, journalists, and institutions that Palestinian lives must be protected and valued equally.

One of the recurring themes in these chapters is the danger of dehumanisation. We see it in media language that frames Palestinian deaths as numbers without names or context, while Israeli deaths are covered through portraits and family stories. We see it in narratives of "human shields" used to justify massive bombardment, despite clear principles of proportionality in international law. And we see it in silence itself: the refusal to centre Palestinian voices, the policing of speech that challenges power, and the erasure of history that explains why Gaza resists and why it suffers.

Yet amid darkness, there are also signs of change. Public opinion, particularly among younger generations, is shifting. Many now see the conflict not as a symmetrical "clash," but as a question of occupation, displacement, and human rights. Movements for a single democratic state with equal rights, once marginal, are gaining attention as the two-state solution recedes into improbability. Artists, academics, and activists, even under threat of censorship or career damage, continue to speak out. And within Gaza itself, the very act of surviving, documenting, and remembering becomes a form of resistance.

The question once thought unthinkable — whether Israel can remain both a Jewish state and a democratic state without permanently denying Palestinian rights — is no longer confined to the margins. This is not to erase Israeli suffering or fears, but to insist that lasting peace cannot be built on the displacement, disenfranchisement, and blockade of millions. Security without justice is neither stable nor moral.

Beyond policy debates, there is an ethical principle at stake: equal protection of all lives. International law was created not to excuse powerful states but to restrain them. When Western governments supply weapons and political cover, they share responsibility for what follows. When the media frames mass killing as unavoidable "collateral damage," they help normalise it. And when citizens remain silent, the machinery of destruction rolls on, unchallenged.

So what does it mean to go beyond silence? It means insisting on naming occupation, apartheid, and possible genocide where evidence compels us. It means challenging double standards that excuse crimes when committed by allies. It means amplifying Palestinian voices and histories too often excluded from official narratives — including the history that begins with the Balfour Declaration's promise, made without the consent of the indigenous people it affected, and the century of dispossession that followed. It means supporting civil society, journalists, lawyers, and human rights defenders who risk their freedom to document and resist. And it means recognising that the question of Gaza is not distant: it is a mirror reflecting global questions about power, justice, and who gets to live safely in this world.

It also requires acknowledging complexity without surrendering to paralysis. Yes, Hamas commits attacks that violate international law, including the killing and kidnapping of civilians. Yes, the conflict is shaped by regional actors, geopolitical rivalries, and internal Palestinian divisions. But these truths do not erase the structural reality: an occupied, blockaded territory whose population bears the brunt of overwhelming military force. Complexity cannot be an excuse for inaction or moral equivalence when the power imbalance is so stark.

Some will ask: What can individuals do? The answer is both limited and profound. We can educate ourselves beyond mainstream headlines, support independent journalism, and listen to those living under siege rather than speaking for them. We can challenge policies of our own governments — through protest, advocacy, and voting — that enable injustice abroad. We can defend freedom of expression so that artists, writers, and activists can speak without fear. And above all, we can refuse to accept that Palestinian lives are worth less.

Hope is a difficult word when so much has been lost. But history shows that what seems permanent can crumble: apartheid in South Africa, segregation in the U.S., and authoritarian regimes once thought untouchable. Change comes not from inevitability, but from pressure, conscience, and collective action. Gaza's catastrophe is not the product of an unstoppable force of history; it is the consequence of choices made and sustained by human beings — and so it can also be changed by human beings.

This book is not offered as the final word or as a neutral account. It takes a side: the side of civilian lives over military objectives, of equality over supremacy, of memory over erasure. It asks readers not merely to feel pity, but to act — by speaking, writing, protesting, and demanding that governments uphold the principles they claim to cherish.

In the end, silence is easy. It is the default path of those who fear controversy, risk, or discomfort. But if we choose to look away from Gaza — from the children drawing hope on ruined walls, from the doctors operating by phone light, from poets censored and refugees displaced again and again — we choose not just to ignore suffering but to help sustain it.

Beyond silence lies responsibility, and beyond responsibility the possibility, however distant, of a future built on justice rather than rubble.

History will not ask whether we were comfortable. It will ask whether we were complicit — or whether, at the hardest moment, we chose to speak.